Praise for
The WholeHearted Wife

What's better than a book with the name "Smalley" on the cover? How about a book with three Smalleys! Erin and Greg, along with Greg's dad, Gary, offer women a powerful message that will help strengthen and reinvigorate their relationships with their husbands. This is a great book for Christian women.

    JIM DALY
    President, Focus on the Family

As a radio host I've talked with a great number of relationship experts but I must say, I've never met a family more committed to the success of your marriage than the Smalleys. They're passionate about your having a marriage that's a safe place for you and a great example for others. If you're a wife and you want to move beyond the status quo, if you long for a strong and thriving marriage, then you've come to the right place. Take your time as you work your way through the pages of this book. Embrace a teachable, hopeful heart as you consider a new approach to your husband. Your story is far from over. God's about to do a new thing in you!

    SUSIE LARSON
    National radio host; speaker
    Author of *Your Beautiful Purpose*

I am so grateful the Smalleys have written this book. These hard-learned lessons will steer all of us to more meaningful relationships and stronger marriages. I love the real-life honesty coupled with big splashes of fun that is shown in this book.

    BRADY BOYD
    Senior Pastor, New Life Church
    Author of *Addicted to Busy*

This book is full of practical advice for women. Let's face it . . . being a wife is far more complicated than most of us realized when we said, "I do." Greg and Erin do an excellent job of equipping you to honor God and your husband, regardless of the current state of your marriage.

> DR. JULI SLATTERY
> Author; clinical psychologist; co-founder of Authentic Intimacy

What a fantastic book! Every wife—regardless of age or stage in her marriage—will benefit from this inspiring, humorous, and practical message.

> DR. LESLIE PARROTT
> Marriage and family therapist
> #1 New York Times best-selling author of *The Good Fight*

The Smalleys bring both professional expertise and personal experience to the important conversation of what it takes to nurture a loving marriage. The Smalleys have successfully combined their humor and personal experience with their expertise from years of marriage ministry, making *The WholeHearted Wife* a great resource for any married couple.

> DR. TONY EVANS
> Pastor of Oak Cliff Bible Fellowship, Dallas, Texas
> Author of *Kingdom Woman*

THE
WHOLEHEARTED WIFE

◇◇◇◇◇◇◇◇◇◇◇ ♥ ♥ ♥ ◇◇◇◇◇◇◇◇◇◇◇

THE WHOLE *hearted*
WIFE

♥ ♥ ♥

10 keys to a
more loving relationship

SMALLEY
ERIN, GREG, AND GARY

INSPIRED BY GARY SMALLEY'S *HIDDEN KEYS TO LOVING RELATIONSHIPS*

TYNDALE HOUSE PUBLISHERS, INC.
CAROL STREAM, ILLINOIS

The Wholehearted Wife: 10 Keys to a More Loving Relationship
© 2014 by Erin Smalley, Greg Smalley, and Gary Smalley

ISBN: 978-1-62405-146-3

A Focus on the Family book published by
Tyndale House Publishers, Inc., Carol Stream, Illinois 60188

Focus on the Family and the accompanying logo and design are federally registered trademarks of Focus on the Family, 8605 Explorer Drive, Colorado Springs, CO 80920.

TYNDALE and Tyndale's quill logo are registered trademarks of Tyndale House Publishers, Inc.

People's names and certain details of their stories have been changed to protect the privacy of the individuals involved. However, the facts of what happened and the underlying principles have been conveyed as accurately as possible.

Excerpts from *Making Love Last Forever* used by permission. Gary Smalley, 1996. Thomas Nelson. Nashville, Tennessee. All rights reserved.

Unless otherwise marked, scripture quotations are from the *Holy Bible, New International Version*® NIV® Copyright © 1973, 1978, 1984 by Biblica, Inc.® Used by permission. All rights reserved worldwide. Scripture quotations marked (NASB) are taken from the *New American Standard Bible*®. Copyright © 1960, 1962, 1963, 1968, 1971, 1972, 1973, 1975, 1977, 1995 by The Lockman Foundation. Used by permission. (www.Lockman.org). Scripture quotations marked (NCV) taken from the *New Century Version*®. Copyright © 2005 by Thomas Nelson, Inc. Used by permission. All rights reserved. Scripture quotations marked (NKJV) are taken from the *New King James Version*®. Copyright © 1982 by Thomas Nelson, Inc. Used by permission. All rights reserved. Scripture quotations marked (NLT) are taken from the *Holy Bible, New Living Translation*, copyright © 1996, 2004, 2007 by Tyndale House Foundation. Used by permission of Tyndale House Publishers, Inc., Carol Stream, Illinois 60188. All rights reserved. Scripture quotations marked (MSG) are taken from *THE MESSAGE* [paraphrase]. Copyright © by Eugene H. Peterson 1993, 1994, 1995, 1996, 2000, 2001, 2002. Used by permission of NavPress Publishing Group. Scripture quotations marked (TLB) are taken from *The Living Bible* [paraphrase], copyright © 1971. Used by permission of Tyndale House Publishers, Inc., Carol Stream, Illinois 60188. All rights reserved. Scriptures marked (Phillips) are taken from J. B. Phillips, *The New Testament in Modern English*, 1962 edition, published by HarperCollins.

Editorial contributors: Lisa Frieden, Jennifer Lonas, and Marianne Hering
Cover design by Jennifer Ghionzoli

Cataloging-in-Publication Data for this book can be found at the Library of Congress website, http://www.loc.gov.

Printed in the United States of America

1   2   3   4   5   6   7   8   9 /19   18   17   16   15   14

To three amazing men in my life:

My dad, Patrick Murphy. We were joined through the gift of adoption and shared loving one amazing woman—Rosalie Antoinette. I am thankful for your constant presence in my life. I love you!

My second dad, Gary Thomas Smalley. Thank you for loving me as your own daughter. Thank you for all you have taught me starting back in chapel at GCU—before I ever imagined I'd marry your son.

My amazing husband, Gregory Thomas Smalley. Thank you for encouraging me to pursue my dreams—truly you have been my "dream maker." You have given me four amazing children—Taylor, Murphy, Garrison, and Annie—three through biology and one through the gift of adoption. Thank you for loving me and the kids wholeheartedly. You are irreplaceable! I love you dearly!

—ERIN SMALLEY

Contents

✦✦✦✦✦✦✦✦✦✦✦ ♥♥♥ ✦✦✦✦✦✦✦✦✦✦

Preface

xxxxxxxxxxxxxxxxxxxxxx ♥ ♥ ♥ xxxxxxxxxxxxxxxxxxxx

For Women Only?

You may be wondering why we've written a book on marriage that's just for women. Great question! As you'll see in the pages that follow, you have the ability to influence the overall temperature of your marriage. You may think that improving your marriage requires your husband's participation. Ideally it does, but even if he isn't motivated to work with you, a stronger, more satisfying marriage is still within reach. Ultimately, the key to a more loving, vibrant relationship with your husband lies in discovering how you can become a wholehearted wife.

You may be reading this book for any number of reasons. Perhaps you have a good marriage, but you want it to be great. You know that even the best marriages encounter challenging times. After all, in the chaos of life, it's easy to grow increasingly disconnected from your husband. So you're reading this book to find ways to reconnect and deepen the love you share.

Some of you may be facing serious disappointment in your marriage. Neither your relationship nor your husband is living up to what you expected. You may be disillusioned over what has unfolded over the years and feel this isn't what you signed up for. You may be worn out and exhausted from caring for an entire family, maybe even working outside the home full-time. You know your marriage needs help, but trying to make even the smallest change can feel impossible and hopeless. Perhaps you have very little desire to work on your marriage at all. You just want out, but you know it shouldn't be that way, and you hope this book will renew your motivation to try again.

For others, your marriage may be in crisis, and this book may be a last-ditch effort to see if there's anything you can do to save your marriage and turn things around. Perhaps you're dealing with serious issues in your marriage such as emotional or physical abuse, addictive behaviors, infidelity, mental illness, or some other damaging or debilitating condition. If you and your husband are struggling with any of these issues in your marriage, we strongly encourage you to talk with a licensed, professional Christian counselor.*

But this book can also help you find hope for change even in the midst of the most difficult circumstances. No matter where you are in your marriage, this book offers encouragement and valuable help for change and growth. Whether you've been married for two weeks or twenty-two years—the keys presented in this book are for you. If you feel helpless and stuck, gazing across an ever-widening chasm in your marital relationship, in these pages you can find the help and hope you need. Or if you think that your marriage is on solid ground, but you refuse to settle for mediocrity, this book can serve as a practical companion and guide as you pursue a more loving relationship with your husband.

As you begin this journey, you might be like I (Erin) was twenty

---

* The Focus on the Family Help Center counselors are here to listen and pray with you, as well as provide guidance and resources to help you and your family thrive. Arrange to speak with a licensed Christian counselor at no cost by calling 1-855-771-HELP (4357) Monday through Friday between 6:00 a.m. and 8:00 p.m. Mountain time. Due to high call volumes, it may be necessary for you to leave your name and number for a counselor to return your call.

years ago, driving down Highway 5 in Southern California to a conference at which "the preacher," now my father-in-law, was speaking. At
this point in my marriage, I was struggling and wanted to hear some
words of encouragement. As I listened halfheartedly to the message,
my mind wandered back to a college chapel service where, many years
earlier, I had listened to the same man speak. What I learned from Gary
Smalley back then had been life changing. And now I was hearing these
same basic concepts again, except this time they were impacting not
only my life but also, ironically, my marriage to his son.

Fast-forward to my marriage today. Thanks to the principles I
learned from Gary Smalley during this earlier crisis point in my marriage, I've seen my marriage relationship change dramatically over the
years. I've also been reminded at various stages of my life to keep practicing these principles. (Somehow, even when we know the truth, we
need regular reminders to believe and live it.) Over many years, Gary
crystallized these core truths about marriage from Scripture and his
experience of working with thousands of married couples. The principles he developed, originally presented in the book and video series
Hidden Keys to Loving Relationships, had a powerful impact on an earlier
generation of married couples. But so many women today haven't been
exposed to these biblical principles combined with common sense that
I first heard Gary Smalley talk about when I was a college student.

The book you're holding in your hands is the culmination of an
effort to ensure that all women, young and old, have the opportunity to
discover how they can experience a more loving relationship with their
husbands. We (Gary, Greg, and I) decided to offer this new book and
curriculum, *The Wholehearted Wife: 10 Keys to a More Loving Relationship*, to help women learn how they can influence their marriages for
good. Our ultimate desire is to see marriages transformed among new
generations of women as they discover the joy of becoming wholehearted wives.

As you read this book, keep in mind that every marriage has three entities: a woman, a man, and the marriage itself. We've written the book with this framework in mind, and we encourage you as you learn each key principle to first consider, "How does this principle apply to me?" Then ask yourself, "How can I use this principle to better love and care for my husband?" Finally, ponder this question: "How can I apply this principle in my marriage?"

We don't expect women to apply the ten key principles in the same way. Every marriage is different and has its own unique challenges and circumstances. But no matter what shape your marriage is in—strong, a bit frayed at the seams, or hanging by a thread—the tried-and-true concepts in this book apply to any married woman in any situation.

As you put the key principles into practice in your marriage and continue applying them in the years to come, we pray that you'll become the wholehearted wife God has called you to be. We also pray that you'll recapture, or perhaps experience for the first time, the vibrant, loving relationship with your husband that you've always wanted.

We welcome you on this life-changing journey!

Introduction

xxxxxxxxxxxxxxxxxxxxxx ♥♥♥ xxxxxxxxxxxxxxxxxxxxxx

The Marriage You've Always Wanted

I (Erin) will never forget that day in 1987. I was attending a late-afternoon chapel service at Grand Canyon University (GCU). As I sat on a wooden pew with my friends, waiting for the service to begin, I glanced around the chapel. I decided the building had to be 1970s vintage—the musty smell and burnt-orange accents gave away its age.

The organist led us in a few ancient gospel hymns, and then this Gary Smalley guy emerged as the speaker. Admittedly I was a little out of my element sitting in an outdated chapel on a Monday afternoon, waiting to hear from a preacher. In my family, God talk had been strictly limited to Sundays. And chapel services had been nonexistent at the University of Arizona, where I'd attended my freshman year. So when I transferred to GCU as a sophomore, my expectations for spiritual enlightenment weren't very high. But the faculty and students at GCU had a passion for God that was unlike anything I'd ever seen. I wasn't quite sure what to make of it.

As Gary Smalley began to talk that day, I listened halfheartedly, mostly thinking about the homework I needed to get done. I was also thinking about the preacher's son named Greg.

Earlier in the week, I was involved in a hilarious prank on Greg, who had fallen asleep in Old Testament theology class. Greg wasn't just sleeping; he was drooling sleeping. His friends encouraged me to "help" him, so I shook him and woke him up from his deep sleep. Actually, I went a little further than that. I whispered to him that the professor had called on him to pray. So very boldly Greg stood up and began to pray right in the middle of the professor's lecture. Everyone in the class burst out laughing, and Greg immediately knew he'd been the brunt of a big joke. At the time he wasn't remotely attractive to me. A drooling, sleeping boy wasn't what I was looking for.

As my mind wandered back to Gary Smalley and his teaching, words and phrases such as *honor*, *closed spirit*, and *anger* caught my attention. I began to listen more intently and embraced the hope that I might actually learn something. And learn I did. This preacher was presenting new concepts about relationships that made so much sense. I especially remember him talking about plugging into the right source of power and satisfaction in our lives. That source wasn't people, circumstances, or things. It was God. The difference between a poor source and the right source, he said, was like a 110-volt outlet versus a high-power 220-volt source. The first one just couldn't provide significant power, and the same was true in our lives. People, circumstances, or possessions could not fill our hearts in any lasting way; real fulfillment, meaning, and power were things only God could provide. As someone who was still trying to figure out what faith was all about, this illustration really hit home. I knew it was true in my own life. Any satisfaction I found never seemed to last. I was beginning to find this preacher guy's advice surprisingly insightful.

That day in chapel I didn't realize how much Gary Smalley's advice would change my life and relationships. I also had no idea that years later I'd be engaged to his son, waiting in another chapel for Gary Smalley himself to perform the wedding ceremony!

Disillusionment Hits Home

I (Erin) can still remember walking down the aisle in my perfect wedding dress—a tulle gown radiating with small, sparkly rhinestones. My best friends were standing at the altar waiting for me to arrive. The program had been set up perfectly, with each minute accounted for. Gary guided us through the ceremony with grace and precision. Soon Greg and I were gazing dreamily into each other's eyes as we said our vows, and before I knew it, he was lifting my veil to kiss me.

Shortly after this perfect ceremony, Greg and I left for our honeymoon. But within hours we realized that marriage wasn't going to be quite as picture-perfect as our wedding.

Think back to your own wedding day. I'm quite sure that when you said "I do," you didn't anticipate feeling any different than you did at that moment. As little girls, we dreamed of our wedding day and planned out every glorious detail—the design of the ring on our finger, the color scheme, the flowers in our bouquet, the style of dress we wanted, and the perfect honeymoon location. We may have imagined a dashing Prince Charming sweeping us off our feet and remaining completely devoted to our happiness forever after. As we gazed into the future, we all had great expectations and hopes of a fulfilling, happy marriage.

Then over months and years of married life, disappointments and unmet expectations chipped away at our wedded bliss. Disillusionment hit home as we noticed the flaws in our husbands—so much so that at times we could see only the negative. The rose-colored lenses through which we once viewed our husbands began to darken. Our idealistic hopes collided with a disappointing reality, and we personally discovered what we may or may not have been told ahead of time: Marriage can be hard! Our natural reaction to disillusionment is to pull away, to disengage from the relationship, to hold back (rather than engaging passionately and wholeheartedly). We may convince ourselves that this is as good as it gets, so we had better accept "reality" and get on with married life, such as it is. But the loss of vitality and passion in our relationship brings with it a heartache that won't go away. Somewhere along the way reality snuffs out the dream of a perfect marriage, and we're left with the feeling that we've been cheated somehow. We wanted a vibrant, loving relationship with our Prince Charming, but we ended up grasping at an illusion that seems to exist only in our dreams. Disillusionment diminishes, dulls, or chips away at an open, free-spirited, and wholehearted expression of love. When we close off our hearts, love begins to wither and dry up. We know that marriage isn't supposed to be this way, but we also know that our childhood dream isn't realistic. The degree of disillusionment varies from marriage to marriage. For some women, the disappointment may be mild, but for others the gap between expectations and reality leaves us with a devastating void in our lives.

When I married Greg, I assumed that this son of Gary Smalley, the renowned relationship expert, would possess all the important tools to be a great husband and guide us into a successful marriage. However, hours into our honeymoon we had our first major argument as husband and wife. And within two years we were on the brink of a separation.

Let me clarify that at the time I was working as a labor-and-delivery nurse, and Greg was a full-time student studying to earn a doctorate in psychology. He was brilliant when it came to working with other people's marriage issues. However, when it came to everything in our relationship, we had a difficult time seeing eye to eye. We had different personalities, different habits, different likes and dislikes. We did laundry differently, spent our free time differently, and had differing opinions.

I can remember coming home from a crazy twelve-hour shift at the hospital and learning that Greg had been out to the movies and lunch with a good friend. Why hadn't he been holding down the fort at home, cleaning up the house, or putting a meal together instead of leaving it all for me to do? I had always encouraged him to do stuff with his friends before we got married, but afterward I didn't feel quite so generous.

Conflict over these and other issues became frequent and mismanaged. Our hearts grew distant and closed toward each other, and each of us began to wonder if we had married the wrong person. How had we come to this perfectly awful place after what seemed like such a perfect wedding?

They say that when a man marries a woman,
he thinks, "She's the one I've been waiting for.
She'll never change"—and she always does.
And a woman looks at her man, and thinks, "He
just needs a little work; after we're married,
I'll help him change"—and he never does.

—Old saying cited in Lauri Przybysz, "Changing
Your Spouse—and Yourself"

A Barrage of Demands

On top of the disillusioning reality that marriage is hard work, I (Erin) soon discovered that married life is incredibly busy. Early on in our marriage, balancing our relationship with work and life's demands was challenging enough. But then we added kids to the mix, and their needs consumed my energy and attention.

I especially remember the season of having three young children when each day drained every ounce of energy I had. I so desired to greet my husband excitedly at the end of his hard workday. However, the reality often was that I felt utterly exhausted, and all I wanted to do was escape the four walls of my home. Usually I ended up going out for coffee with a girlfriend who was also battling the same exhaustion. And occasionally Greg and I would get a babysitter so we could make time for us to connect—but not nearly as often as we would have liked.

Now those three kids are in elementary school, high school, and college. But as God in His sense of humor would have it, I'm the mother of a preschooler again through the gift of adoption—this time in my mid-forties—and once again I'm always tired. I wake up in the morning dreaming of the long run I'll take, the quiet moments I'll enjoy on my deck gazing at the majestic view of Pikes Peak, or the intimate conversations about life I'll savor with a girlfriend over coffee. But somehow most days don't go that way. Life's realities—a sick child, a clogged toilet, an unanticipated car repair—along with daily demands often make me feel weary and worn out.

The good news is that I have more focus and experience to help me out this time around—not to mention better vitamins. I also have a clearer vision for how to approach my marriage.

Sometimes I actually do stop to remind myself to connect with Greg and nurture our marriage. But there are times it feels like just one more thing to add to the to-do list—along with cleaning the house, making dinner, doing laundry, and getting multiple children to sports practice on time. And, oh yes, somewhere in there I'm supposed to be intimate with my husband.

If you're anything like me, by the end of the day, you've given, given, given to everyone else and have nothing left to give. Let's face it, as married women we often encounter a barrage of demands. Is it any wonder that exhaustion and hopelessness can set in, causing us to lose motivation to improve our marriages? And the longer such circumstances drag on, the more our initial desire to try harder can dissipate. We know we need to nurture more loving relationships with our husbands, but often we just want to fall into bed each night and sleep soundly.

We're not alone in feeling this way. Consider these statistics:

- The majority of working Americans say they don't have time for the most important relationships in their lives.[1]
- Since 1973, leisure time in America has decreased by about 20 percent.[2]
- A 2012 survey conducted by the American Psychological Association (APA) titled "Stress in America" indicated that almost half of all women surveyed reported an increase of stress in the past five years.[3]

Without a doubt, American life is busy and stressful, especially for the typical married woman.

Yet in spite of all our busyness, the desire for loving relationships doesn't go away. And it shouldn't. As women we often define ourselves by the quality of our relationships. Typically, the quality relationship every married woman wants most—the one she dreamed about when she walked down the aisle in her white dress—is with her spouse. As busy, stressed-out married women whose dreams collided with reality, we may wonder whether that kind of relationship is even possible. Let me assure you it is!

Jesus said He came so that we might "have life, and have it to the full" (John 10:10). Isn't this what we're longing for in our marriages—a full life and a vibrant love? Married life may not resemble the life of our dreams. In fact, most likely it won't. Jesus didn't come to fulfill our dreams of the good life. But He did promise us a full life.

So how can we experience that kind of life and love in our marriages? I know for sure that it doesn't come by living on autopilot. No dream or worthy goal comes easily. We must *intentionally pursue* what matters most in our lives and marriages.

Your Influence Can Make All the Difference

Perhaps you feel powerless to improve your marriage because you know it "takes two" for real change to take place. I (Erin) couldn't agree more. It does take two committed individuals to improve a marriage. However, I also believe that we as women often sell ourselves short when it comes to the overall impact we can have on our marriages. Instead of minimizing our role, we need to embrace an important truth: *As women we can greatly influence the state of our marriages.* Let me say very carefully here that we cannot (and shouldn't try to) *control* our marriages, or our husbands, but we can *influence* them. The word *influence* means "the capacity . . . to produce effects on the actions, behavior, [and] opinions of others."[4]

What the Bible Says About Influence

No marriage book or counsel can guarantee the outcome of a relationship. But the counsel of God regarding marriage is true and sure: The growth of one person in a marriage relationship impacts the other person. Scripture indicates this is true even when one partner in the marriage isn't a follower of Christ. Take, for example, Paul's encouragement to spouses in the church at Corinth, which was filled with struggling believers living in a morally decadent city:

> If a Christian woman has a husband who is not a believer, and he is happy to live with her, she must not divorce him. The husband who is not a believer is made holy through his believing wife. And the wife who is not a believer is made holy through her be-

> lieving husband. If this were not true, your children
> would not be clean, but now your children are holy.
> (1 Corinthians 7:13–14, NCV)

And the apostle Peter, also speaking to wives whose husbands were not following God, reminded them that their godly lives would speak louder than words as an influence upon their husbands. A godly life is, in fact, the best means of influencing a marriage. Peter expressed it this way:

> Wives, fit in with your husbands' plans; for then if they
> refuse to listen when you talk to them about the Lord,
> they will be won by your respectful, pure behavior.
> Your godly lives will speak to them better than any
> words. (1 Peter 3:1-2, TLB)

The most effective way we can positively influence our marriages is by changing what we *can* control: ourselves. We can control our attitudes, our actions, our decisions, our priorities, and even our words. This happens, however, only through the power of the Holy Spirit. He alone can change the human heart—from which all of our behaviors, choices, and responses flow. Our goal, then, as women must be to first deal with ourselves.

I (Erin) love how Linda Dillow differentiates a goal from a desire in her book *What's It Like to Be Married to Me?*

A goal is a purpose to which a woman is unalterably committed. She assumes unconditional responsibility for a goal,
and it can be achieved if she is willing to work at it. A desire
is something wanted that cannot be obtained without the

cooperation of another person. It is an objective for which a person can assume no responsibility because it is beyond her control. Reaching a desire must never become the motivating purpose behind behavior, because then a person is assuming responsibility for something she cannot fulfill on her own. *A goal is something I want that I can also control. A desire is something I want that I cannot control.* [Emphasis added.][5]

We may desire a more vibrant, loving, and intimate marriage, but as Linda so eloquently expressed it, we must never make a desire "the motivating purpose behind [our] behavior." Why? Because it's beyond our control. In essence, if we want a more loving relationship with our husbands, we must first pursue the goal of becoming more loving, God-focused wives.

It took me a long while to grasp that and be willing to turn to God for His help. I've had to make choices about doing chores cheerfully instead of nagging Greg to do them. I've had to make a choice of how I would respond to him when he walks in the door at "the bewitching hour"—you know, 5 p.m. when everyone needs help with homework, you're trying to fix dinner, the baby is fussy, and the kids are rushing out the door to sports practice. Would I ignore him? Would I treat him as one more demand on my already full plate? Would I nag him to not just stand there but pitch in (can't he see what needs to be done!)? Or would I pause for a moment, set everything aside, and greet him with a kiss? Both types of responses set a tone and sent a message to my husband. And both tended to influence our marriage and his response to me. God helped me see that making these kinds of choices begin in *my* heart and greatly affect our marriage.

The same is true for you. No matter what your relationship looks like or how you feel about it, we want you to know there's hope. You truly can make a difference in your marriage by becoming the woman and wife God intends you to be.

A More Loving Relationship Begins with You

Often in marriage we become very aware of our spouses' problematic attitudes and behaviors, and we think our input, directly or subtly, can fix them. Believe me, I (Erin) have tried with all my might to let Greg know that he should stop watching so much television, or work a little less, or put his dishes in the dishwasher. I've often done this indirectly or covertly. But when my subtle input didn't work, I would get frustrated and feel like giving up because I knew I couldn't change him.

I used to say things like, "I can't change Greg. He's going to do what he's going to do." But then the Lord would say ever so gently to me, "No, you can't change him . . . but I can. And I can also change *you*." Ouch.

Honestly, it was much easier and more fun—and self-justifying—to talk about Greg and what he was or wasn't doing in our relationship. That definitely kept the focus off me—but ultimately it kept me from growing as a person. It kept me from having to take a long, hard look in the mirror.

Many of the things I disliked about Greg pointed to things I disliked about myself. But I couldn't see those things until I stopped and looked. Learning to focus on my own flaws and the ways God wants to change me has been an ongoing process. But I've gradually come to realize that I can't change my husband or anyone else. I can focus only on myself and cooperate with God as He changes my heart.

That's really the bottom line for married women: *A more loving relationship with our spouses begins with us.* It begins with the realization that ultimately we cannot change our spouses. We can, however, take a penetrating look at ourselves and ask, "How can I become the best wife I can be? How can I approach my relationship with my husband differently? What can I do to nurture a more vibrant, loving relationship with him?"

A wise woman knows that it's not her words, but her behavior that carries the biggest clout when it comes to compelling change. The more Christlike you are, the more positive your influence will be. If you truly want to influence someone else for good, you won't focus on changing his behavior. You'll focus on changing your behavior. You'll work at becoming more godly, and on interacting in a more godly way.

—Mary Kassian, *Girls Gone Wise in a World Gone Wild*

Becoming a Wholehearted Wife

Once we've embraced the truth that a more loving relationship with our spouses begins with us, we may find that our hearts aren't all that thrilled about taking the first steps toward change. In fact, the condition of our hearts is often the first change that needs to take place. Change, like love, is a matter of the will, but it also involves the heart. And heart-level change doesn't happen overnight. It takes time.

Disillusionment and broken dreams may have caused us to wrap our hearts in a thick, self-protective layer of armor. Our hearts may have been closed off from our husbands for years. Hurt and resentment may have grown deep roots. We may long for a more loving relationship with our husbands, but before we can truly open our hearts again, the armor needs to be stripped away, and our stony hearts need to soften. For many of us, letting down our guard and softening our hearts may seem impossible. Thankfully, we belong to a God who is a heart specialist. Just as He alone can change the hearts of our spouses, He alone can change our hearts.

An amazing thing happens when we allow God to change our hearts. He fills us with His unconditional love and enables us to reach out to our husbands wholeheartedly without demands or preconditions. Romans 5:5 reminds us that "God has poured out his love into our hearts by the Holy Spirit." As we focus on becoming more like Jesus, the fruit of His Spirit will grow in our hearts, and His love will flow through us to influence our marriages and our spouses (Galatians 5:22). God's love has the power to transform even the most hopeless relationship. This is the secret of becoming a wholehearted wife.

In Ephesians 6:7, the apostle Paul tells us to "serve wholeheartedly, as if you were serving the Lord, not men." I believe that God is calling us to serve wholeheartedly, not only at work and in ministry but also in our marriages. Being wholehearted means giving ourselves fully in every aspect of our relationships with our spouses, not out of a sense of duty, but because we're ultimately serving the Lord. Loving and serving wholeheartedly involve the whole person—spiritually, emotionally, mentally, and physically.

Let me clarify, however, that just as there are no perfect marriages this side of heaven, there are no perfectly wholehearted wives. But as we become more Christlike, we will love our husbands more wholeheartedly, and when we fail or fall short, we can ask God to forgive us and empower us once again to devote ourselves fully to Him and our spouses.

To be wholehearted wives, we can't invest ourselves halfheartedly in our marriages. Loving wholeheartedly means engaging fully in our marriages and seeking the best for our husbands. When disillusionment and shattered dreams threaten to diminish our love, we must resist the temptation to pull away, disengage, or give up. We must guard against closing off our hearts self-protectively when disappointments come and promises are broken.

Ultimately, we must entrust our marriages into God's care and trust wholeheartedly in His ability transform them. No matter what your relationship with your husband is like right now, take heart! As you learn the keys to a more loving relationship, God will mold you into the wholehearted wife He intends you to be. So let's get started!

⬥⬥⬥⬥⬥⬥⬥⬥⬥⬥⬥⬥⬥⬥⬥ ♥♥♥ ⬥⬥⬥⬥⬥⬥⬥⬥⬥⬥⬥⬥⬥⬥

The Value of a Diamond

One momentous day in third grade, our (Greg and Erin's) daughter Murphy came home from school with a flyer that had caught her attention. She had learned that day about Crater of Diamonds State Park located in Murfreesboro, Arkansas, approximately a five-hour drive from our home. The brochure highlighted the fact that this park is the only diamond-producing site in the world that's open to the public. Visitors are welcome to search for diamonds and keep whatever they find. In fact, at this park someone had discovered a forty-carat diamond. Murphy had read all this in the brochure and was captivated. She begged and pleaded for us to go hunting for diamonds. We had to admit it did sound pretty interesting.

Memorial Day wasn't too far off, and it turned out that some friends not far from Murfreesboro had invited us to their cabin for the weekend. Perfect! We could make an adventure of it—and maybe even strike it rich. So in great anticipation we piled into the car for the five-hour drive, met our friends at their cabin, and got up early the next morning to begin our quest for diamonds.

Well, it was what the brochure *didn't* say that set the tone for the day. Crater of Diamonds State Park is a thirty-seven-acre, barren wasteland. Dirty. Dusty. Hot. Humid. Nasty! We discovered that we had to rent shovels, sifters, and buckets just to begin our search for diamonds. Then we were told to simply pick anywhere we wanted and start digging. Every shovelful went into a sifter. Next, we had to shake the sifter until we found any little nugget bigger than a pebble. Then we had to sift again, this time in water that just got dirtier and dirtier. If we thought a tiny nugget looked as if it might be a diamond, we were told to take it to the evaluator.

Needless to say, it didn't take long in the sweltering heat and muck for us all to discover that this treasure hunt wasn't what we had envisioned. Twenty minutes into the shoveling, bucket dumping, and sifting, the kids were crying—and on the inside so was I (Erin). I can clearly remember the sweat accumulating around my feet as the perspiration ran down every part of my body, collecting dusty grime along the way.

After an hour of strenuous work, none of us had found a thing. What a contrast to the treasure hunt we had anticipated. We had embarked on this adventure with high hopes. We had devoted an awful lot of resources—gas, travel, time, and hard work—just for the chance to unearth a diamond we could bring home and proudly display. Murphy—and the rest of us—valued diamonds. You might say that in our minds they held a place of honor.

Honoring what we deeply value and cherish is one of the most vital principles in marriage. I (Gary) have spoken around the world to thousands of couples and have written numerous best-selling books on relationships. And to this day I still consider the idea of honor essential for a successful marriage. In fact, honor is foundational to all other relationship-building principles you'll ever learn. This concept appears in almost all of my books and in virtually all of my marriage videos.

Marital expert Dr. John Gottman agrees that honor (or admiration) is one of the most important aspects of a healthy marital relationship:

Admiration [is one] of the most crucial elements in a rewarding and long-lasting romance. Although happily married couples may feel driven to distraction at times by their partner's personality flaws, they still feel that the person they married is worthy of honor and respect.[1]

The fact that honor is an essential ingredient in relationships is no surprise, since Scripture states that God Himself deserves our honor (1 Samuel 2:30; Revelation 4:11; 5:12–13), and the Ten Commandments include the command to honor (Exodus 20:12). The apostle Paul also emphasized the importance of expressing honor in relationships: "Be devoted to one another in . . . love. *Honor one another above yourselves*" (Romans 12:10, emphasis added).

Honor is "a decision expressed by placing high value, worth, and importance on another person."[2] It's essentially an attitude you hold toward your husband.[3] It means viewing your husband as a "priceless diamond" and granting him a "highly respected position" in your life.[4] Closely related to honor is the concept of cherishing. Like honor, cherishing is an attitude that conveys deep value and high regard.

◇◇

Marriage should be honored by all.

—Hebrews 13:4

◇◇

Sometimes it's difficult for us to affirm our husbands' value because we feel worthless and devalued ourselves. We may have grown up in an abusive home or lacked the nurturing love we so desperately needed as children. Or other life experiences may have beaten us down and made us feel flawed or unlovable. Whatever the case may be, the first step in learning to honor our husbands often involves understanding and embracing our own value in God's eyes.

Embracing Your Value

Have you ever wandered through a maze of mirrors at a House of Mirrors carnival attraction? The curved and elongated mirrors are designed to reflect distorted images when you stand in front of them. The mirrors can make you look short, tall, thin, fat, funny, weird, crazy, or scary depending on how the image is distorted.

Like a house of mirrors, the world we live in is filled with distorted images. When Adam and Eve's perfect world was destroyed, we inherited from them a fallen, sin-stained world. Every aspect of our culture, including TV shows, movies, and magazines, presents a distorted image of reality. Not even the things we consider good or normal in today's world come close to God's original flawless design.

And if that isn't bad enough, we also have to contend with an enemy, "the father of lies" (John 8:44), who relentlessly tries to twist the truth about who we are. No wonder it often feels as if we're living in a crazy house of mirrors!

What do you see when you look in the mirror? Does your image look warped, or does it reflect the truth about how God created you?

You might wonder why this matters, but the fact is, how we view ourselves directly impacts how we view our husbands. In fact, *we can't adequately love and honor our husbands unless we love ourselves and understand our value in God's sight.* The second greatest commandment tells us to "love your neighbor as yourself" (Mark 12:31). The assumption is that we already love ourselves, but many of us struggle with doing just that because we don't understand our value.

If we want to see a true reflection of our value, we need to look at ourselves in God's mirror. Consider these truths from the Bible that declare how much your heavenly Father cherishes you:

- He knit you together in your mother's womb and knows everything about you (Psalm 139:1, 13).

- You are "precious and honored" in His sight (Isaiah 43:4).
- He knew you even before you were conceived (Jeremiah 1:5).
- He takes "great delight" in you and rejoices "over you with singing" (Zephaniah 3:17).
- You are more valuable to Him than "many sparrows" (Matthew 10:29).
- Nothing can ever separate you from His love (Romans 8:39).
- He has "lavished" His love on you and calls you His child (1 John 3:1).

Even if you were the only person on earth, God would have sent His Son to die for you. You're that precious to Him! The apostle Peter described God's amazing love in these words:

> For you know that God paid a ransom to save you from the empty life you inherited from your ancestors. And the ransom he paid was not mere gold or silver. It was the precious blood of Christ, the sinless, spotless Lamb of God. God chose him as your ransom long before the world began. (1 Peter 1:18–20, NLT)

But for some of us, really feeling valuable and loved is difficult, and we may need to take some specific steps to re-train our minds to see God's view of us rather than a distorted one. Christian counselor Robert McGee addressed this issue of grasping your great personal worth in his popular best seller *The Search for Significance*. McGee recommends writing the following truths on a three-by-five-inch card to remind us of our value in Christ:[5]

1. I am deeply loved by God (1 John 4:9–10).
2. I am completely forgiven and am fully pleasing to God (Romans 5:1).
3. I am totally accepted by God (Colossians 1:21–22).
4. I am a new creation, complete in Christ (2 Corinthians 5:17).

Embracing your personal value is so important to a healthy marriage that we (Greg and Gary) devoted an entire chapter to it in *Winning Your Husband Back Before It's Too Late*. In the chapter "Looking in the Mirror . . . Becoming Whole," we reminded women that they must become secure in their identity in Christ and confident of their unique worth in Him.[6]

If your identity isn't rooted in Christ, you may try to draw all your worth from your husband—a need he can never meet. Or you may believe that your worth is based on fulfilling your husband's expectations. This makes your worth dependent on your husband's viewpoint rather than on God's.

Author BeNeca Ward illustrates this in her book *Third Generation Country*:

> My mother sat me down and said, . . . "True beauty is in the eye of the beholder, which means that how beautiful you are to other people is always going to be subjective." . . . She went on to tell me that I needed to . . . identify [and] celebrate what I thought was [beautiful or] weird or unusual [about me] because God had given . . . me [those special things to make] me different from everybody else. I learned how to appreciate, embrace, and enhance those special things so that they would shine rather than be hidden.[7]

Take a few minutes right now to consider your life and answer these important questions:

1. How do I honestly see myself?
2. What do I value about myself?
3. What is God's design for me?
4. How did God uniquely create me?
5. What special gifts and talents has God given me?

Here are a few of the characteristics I (Erin) value about the way God designed me:

1. I'm highly relational. I love being with and relating to people—especially other women.
2. I love to help others when they are hurting—both physically and emotionally (which is why I became a nurse and a counselor).
3. I live life passionately and wholeheartedly. I love deeply, rejoice greatly, and grieve losses sincerely.
4. I have a deep faith in the Lord, and I love to worship in very traditional ways.
5. I'm adventurous and love to try new things.

So what's on your list? God has beautifully and creatively designed you, so thank Him for the unique gifts and abilities He has given you. Let those "special things" shine! And remember: When you embrace your own value in God's sight, you'll gain a greater understanding of your husband's value and a deeper desire to honor him.

Honoring Your Husband

One of the best illustrations of what it means to honor your husband is an analogy I (Gary) used when I was speaking at a large marriage conference. A friend of mine had loaned me an old, beat-up violin for making a point. Several of the strings were missing, and the one that was still there was actually hanging off, attached only on one end of the violin. There was little of the polish or brilliance you might see from a professionally owned instrument.

I passed the violin around so the audience could see it. At first it moved along pretty quickly from person to person. But when I pointed out that the word *Stradivarius*, though faded, was etched inside the violin, the room instantly came alive with oohs and aahs. All of a sudden, this battered violin took on a whole new level of significance. It was valuable! After all, many Stradivarius violins, made in the seventeenth and eighteenth centuries, are valued at more than a million dollars.[8] The violin was passed around slowly and carefully after that comment. Its value had been recognized. This is what honor conveys.

The most powerful way to honor your husband is to recognize and affirm his immense value. Remember the way the audience reacted when they realized the old violin was a Stradivarius? Now imagine yourself oohing or aahing when your husband walks into the room. This may sound a bit ridiculous, but if you really choose to view your husband as a valuable treasure, a precious gift from God, your attitude toward him will reflect this. Treating him as someone you deeply value and cherish will also make it easier to put legs on the idea of loving him, especially when it's difficult. In many cases, love begins to flow when you've made the choice to honor your husband.

◇◇

> *How we handle our husband's short comings reveals more about our own character than our [husband's].*
>
> —Courtney Joseph, Women Living Well Ministries

◇◇

At times you may not feel like honoring your spouse. But here's the good news: The choice to honor your husband is just that—a choice. You can choose to treat your husband as if he's a priceless treasure—a Stradivarius or a twenty-four-carat diamond—regardless of your feelings. You can choose to treat him with respect simply because he's your husband, whether or not you agree with everything he does.

How do you view your husband? As an old, beat-up violin or as a Stradivarius? How do you treat him? Like a worthless pebble or a twenty-four-carat diamond you've just unearthed?

Ephesians 5:33 says, "The wife must respect her husband." Note that the apostle Paul didn't qualify this statement. He didn't say, "Respect your husband as long as he deserves your respect." God has placed husbands in a leadership position in the marriage, and for that reason alone, wives are called to respect and honor them.

This doesn't mean you must honor your husband's negative qualities or shortcomings. Rather, truthfully focus on those qualities you value and admire.[9] This is in keeping with Philippians 4:8:

Whatever is true, whatever is noble, whatever is right, whatever is pure, whatever is lovely, whatever is admirable—if anything is excellent or praiseworthy—think about such things.

Honor affirms what is true, noble, right, pure, lovely, and admirable. That's why it's so important to affirm with words and actions the good we see in our husbands. When we choose to recognize their immense value and treat them like priceless treasures, we're honoring them. This is what Romans 12:10 (NASB) calls us to do: "Give preference to one another in honor."

Another way we can honor our husbands is by recognizing and valuing the differences in our relationship. Differences can sometimes cause great irritation in a marriage, but they can also spice things up and stimulate growth. In essence, how spouses handle their differences can determine in great part whether a marriage will succeed or fail.

I (Gary) have been speaking and writing about gender differences for more than thirty years. The following are a few of the key differences I've discovered through decades of research and observation. See if you recognize any of these differences in your marriage:[10]

Men . . .

- love to share facts;
- tend to connect by doing things with others;

- tend to be very competitive and task oriented;
- usually find their identity through their accomplishments;

Women . . .

- love to express feelings;
- tend to connect by talking;
- tend to be relationally motivated and focused on cooperation;
- usually find their identity through their relationships.

It's true that generalizations like these don't always apply across the board. But in my experience, they're accurate about 70 to 80 percent of the time.

My point is this: You honor your spouse when you *value* his differences instead of despising them or viewing them as irritants. One way to honor your husband's differences is to make a list of the God-given things you admire about him. In fact, recognizing that these traits are part of the way God designed your husband is another way to praise God! Making a list of positive characteristics can also help restore honor where it has been lacking in your relationship.

Here are a few of the things I (Erin) value about the way God designed Greg:

1. He has a laid-back personality and a great sense of humor. I've especially appreciated this trait when I've run into immobile objects with our vehicles, including the closed garage door, the movie drop box in the McDonald's drive-through line, a pole in a dark parking lot, and his dad's truck, which was parked right behind me in the driveway.

2. He's generous and giving to those in need—including our family! As a dad he's always willing to help our kids with their homework, spending hours assisting them with difficult assignments. He'll even step into arts-and-crafts mode when necessary.

3. He not only recognizes my gifts and abilities (like writing and speaking), but he also encourages me to develop them.

4. He always takes good care of me and our family. I experienced this in a new way as I started writing this book. When I was awakened by intense, severe pain one night, Greg jumped right into crisis mode. He carried me to the recliner and slept on the floor next to me (after I refused to go to the emergency room—I'm such a good nurse!). The next morning he canceled his meetings, took me to the emergency room, and held our family together while I was in the hospital. Throughout the entire ordeal, he showed a new level of caring for me.

5. He prays over me every night before bedtime. Hearing these affirming words at the end of a long day is such a blessing to me!

I smiled, laughed, and cried as I wrote my list. It represented an intentional effort to see the positive qualities in my husband. At times those qualities have caused some frustration in our relationship. For example, although his laid-back personality has been a blessing and relief whenever I've had run-ins with immobile objects, sometimes I want him to get feisty over something I'm feeling feisty about. You know what I mean? "Join me in my drama. Don't calm me!" But the great news is that Greg balances me.

There's always a flip side to each personality trait, so I have to choose whether to view Greg's traits in a positive or negative light. How will you view your husband's traits?

Now it's your turn to list some of the things you admire about your spouse.

1.

2.

3.

4.

When you're finished with your list, share it with your husband. That's another way to honor him!

Honoring your husband and choosing to focus on his positive qualities can have a powerful impact on your relationship. Listen to Lisa's story:

When I married Brad, he was already years into a busy and demanding career at a Fortune 500 company. The expectations for performance were high, and he felt the weight of them. His pressured work demands meant long evenings that left me alone with our kids a lot. I enjoyed my role, but over time I began to resent his preoccupation with work, the constant stress he would talk about, and his seeming indifference to the ordinary but important issues I was dealing with at home each day.

Then one day as I was listening to a Christian radio broadcast, the cohosts challenged listeners to make a list of five or ten qualities we loved about our spouses and thank God for them every day for two weeks. I was so frustrated at that point in our marriage that I could only think of two positive qualities. But I decided that every day I would go to the spare room in our basement, get down on my knees, and thank God out loud for those two things.

The first day I slipped out of bed before my husband was awake and quietly headed downstairs. As an act of the will— certainly not because of any warm fuzzy feelings—I voiced my thanks to God. The next day I did the same. By the third day I was actually able to expand my thanks, citing specific ways I was seeing those qualities in action. In the second week the icy coldness around my heart had begun to thaw. I began to appreciate what he was doing and to realize anew that he had more really great traits I had been overlooking.

I learned from this prayer challenge that making a choice to be thankful for my husband and recognizing his good qualities could actually lead to a change in my heart. Honoring my husband this way didn't solve all of our marital problems, but it certainly changed how I felt about him.

How to Honor Your Husband When He's Behaving Badly

Greg Smalley

1. Separate out the *person* from the *behavior*. Your husband is worthy of honor regardless of his behavior simply because God created him, like you, as a valuable person.

2. Recognize your perception of your husband is impacted by his poor behavior. It's easy to "switch lenses" when you're constantly hurt, fearful, or frustrated by your spouse's negative behavior. Consequently you may see everything through a negative lens. When this happens, you'll tend to notice only his negative behaviors and overlook the positive. Psychologists call this confirmation bias. The solution is to actively look for the positives. This will balance out the tendency to focus on the negatives.

3. Make sure you consider how you might be distorting the problem. You might have a hot button, a pet peeve, an old wound, or an issue in your family of origin that makes a particular behavior loom large in your mind.

4. Confront just the negative behavior—not the person— using healthy conflict-resolution tools. (See my book *Fight Your Way to a Better Marriage* for a practical discussion of how to navigate conflict in a healthy way.)

It's amazing what God can do when we choose to honor our spouses and focus on their positive qualities! If you want to have a more loving relationship with your husband, remember that he's a gift from God, a treasured possession—just as you are. As a wholehearted wife, seek to honor him each day by cherishing him and affirming his value. Treat him like a Stradivarius!

Cherishing Your Marriage

So far we've talked about embracing our own value and honoring our husbands as precious gifts. But it's also important to realize that our *marriages* are valuable as well. Marriage is God's idea. After all, the Bible begins with a marriage (Genesis 2:24) and ends with a marriage (Revelation 19:7–9). Jesus even performed His first miracle at a wedding (John 2:1–11).

Throughout the Scriptures, the metaphor of a bride and groom is used to describe the relationship between God and Israel and Christ and the church (Jeremiah 2:2; Hosea; Ephesians 5:22–33). In Malachi 2:16, when God said, "I hate divorce," He was declaring His passionate love for marriage. One of our favorite verses is Hebrews 13:4: "Marriage should be honored by all." God intensely values marriage and wants us all to do the same. He created the sacred union between you and your husband, and He cares deeply about it.

As individuals, you and your husband matter. But you are more than just the sum of two parts. You're a marriage *team*, and your *oneness* is of great worth. "For this reason a man shall leave his father and his mother, and be joined to his wife; and they shall become one flesh" (Genesis 2:24, NASB).

Over the years many scholars and researchers have studied the importance of marriage, and they've discovered some astonishing advantages. The Heritage Foundation, a conservative think tank in Washington, DC, compiled and published one such list, which includes the following benefits of marriage:

- Married people tend to experience less depression and fewer problems with alcohol.[11]
- Getting married increases the probability of moving out of a poor neighborhood.[12]
- Being married increases the likelihood of affluence.[13]
- Married people are more likely to volunteer.[14]
- Marriage is associated with a lower mortality risk.[15]
- Married couples report greater sexual satisfaction.[16]

So what are some of the things you value about the unique partnership you and your husband share? The list for Greg and me (Erin) includes the following:

1. Because of problems we encountered early on, as well as our unique upbringings, we've become passionate together about strengthening marriages.
2. We have fun and laugh with each other.
3. We share a spiritual relationship.
4. We enjoy raising our children together.
5. We're glad that we are riding life's roller coaster together. We're on an amazing shared adventure!

Now it's your turn. What do you cherish most about your marriage?

1.
2.
3.
4.
5.

Doesn't cherishing your marriage this way make you want to *do* something to express how much your marriage and your husband mean to you? Actions naturally flow from an attitude of honoring and cherishing what we deeply value. That's the theme of our next chapter.

Now that we've explored what it means to embrace our own value, to honor our husbands as precious gifts from God, and to cherish our marriages, we're well on our way toward experiencing more loving relationships with our spouses.

Are you ready to put honor into action?

Key Two: Nourishing

∞∞∞∞∞∞∞∞∞∞∞∞∞∞∞∞∞∞∞ ♥ ♥ ♥ ∞∞∞∞∞∞∞∞∞∞∞∞∞∞∞∞∞∞∞

Honor in Action

If *honoring* is an attitude, *nourishing* is an action. The Bible reminds us that our actions reveal what's in our hearts. How we act will either prove what we say or show that our words are just empty talk.

Consider the following scriptures:

Let us not love with words or tongue but with actions and in truth. (1 John 3:18)

Do not merely listen to the word, and so deceive yourselves. Do what it says. (James 1:22)

Honoring our spouses involves viewing them as priceless treasures, but nourishing takes honor a step further. Nourishing actively expresses honor in tangible ways. It's the process of helping our husbands feel loved, cared for, and valued. *The Free Dictionary* defines the word *nourish* as "[providing] food or other substances necessary for life and growth." When we nourish our husbands, ourselves, and others, we're essentially assisting or providing what is needed to live and grow as individuals and marriage partners.

Scripture refers to this concept when it compares caring for a spouse to "nourishing" our own body (Ephesians 5:29) or describes the tender way in which a mother cares for or "nourishes" her children (1 Thessalonians 2:7). Nourish is the idea of communicating love or fostering the growth of someone with tender, gentle care. These verses aren't addressing wives; in fact, the first one occurs in a short passage to husbands, but it points out a truth that applies to us all: we *naturally* take care of our bodies. We don't cause them pain, but instead are pretty attentive to our bodies' needs (think hunger, sleep, thirst, comfort). It is this kind and regular attentiveness that is conveyed in the biblical idea of nourishing.

So we see that concept of nourishing can be applied in all our relationships—with our spouses, our children, our extended families, and our friends. It essentially describes how we can love others well, caring for them in tangible ways through affirming words and actions. However, as women, we sometimes overexert energy caring for others while not caring for ourselves in a healthy way. God calls us to self-sacrifice but not to self-destruct—and we will explore that difference as we move into this chapter. In my (Erin's) conversations with women, this seems to be a difficult area to navigate.

I know in my own life, I experience stress at times and struggle to balance caring for my own needs with caring for Greg and our children. However, I've learned that we cannot export what we do not import. In other words, we cannot give what we do not have. Thus, to nourish others well—to love them wholeheartedly, especially our husbands—we must first be abundantly full of God's love and have taken care of ourselves. Taking care of ourselves is the job we have been given—no one else can do it for us. Others can assist us, as we do for our spouses—which we will talk about in the section following "Nourishing Yourself." But learning to care for ourselves is ultimately our responsibility—and without fulfilling it we really can't love wholeheartedly.

Nourishing Yourself

Years ago at a family camp, I (Erin) remember sharing with a group of women the idea of taking care of ourselves. Afterward, a woman in her seventies came up and mentioned that the ladies in her church had formed a club called the Yes Girls. Their goal was to always say yes when someone had a need—no wasn't an option. Tears filled her eyes as she described how, one by one, the women dropped out of the club from exhaustion. She explained that no one had ever taught them how to replenish their weary souls. They just gave and gave until emptiness overwhelmed them.

Churches today are littered with burned-out women who have tried to meet every need and demand but end up feeling resentful or like utter failures. As women, many of us struggle with taking care of ourselves. The daily demands of life inundate us, leaving us little time for the self-care we so desperately need. We may wonder whether nourishing ourselves is selfish, or we may not even know how to care for our own needs. Perhaps we've never seen examples of healthy self-care or don't believe we're worth being nourished.

But as we discovered in the previous chapter, each of us is precious to God. Like treasured diamonds, we're of immense value in His sight. Did you know that God even calls us His daughters (Isaiah 43:6–7; 2 Corinthians 6:18)? We have amazing worth simply because we're daughters of the King!

When we truly grasp our value in God's eyes, we can take care of ourselves in a way that honors Him. We'll engage in self-care without being preoccupied with our own happiness and needs. And as needs arise in our lives, we'll be able to entrust them to God (1 Peter 5:7).

Nourishing ourselves is not only necessary for our own health and well-being, but it also enables us to better nourish our husbands and marriages. In the pages that follow, we'll explore what biblical self-care looks like.

Is Self-Care Biblical?

In the previous chapter, we looked at the second greatest commandment as it relates to valuing ourselves. When Jesus said, "Love your neighbor as yourself" (Mark 12:31), He assumed that we already love and care for ourselves. This command doesn't condemn or criticize self-care. Rather, the implied truth is that we love others out of the *fullness* of our love for ourselves. This is why we shouldn't feel guilty about nourishing ourselves. Caring for ourselves enables us to lead lives as wholehearted wives that are full and productive in all the ways that really matter.

As we learn what it means to nourish ourselves, we'll look to the greatest commandment: "Love the Lord your God with all your heart and with all your soul and with all your mind and with all your strength" (Mark 12:30). The four *ways* we're commanded to love God—with our *hearts*, *souls*, *minds*, and *strength*—are also practical aspects of loving and nourishing ourselves. We're called to love God above all other relationships, including ourselves (Matthew 10:37; Luke 14:26). We can also find a four-step model for healthy self-care inside this command.

1. Caring for Your Soul

The first and most crucial aspect of self-care, based on the greatest commandment, is caring for our souls—the spiritual component of our lives. (You might be thinking that this is out of order, but due to the critical role it plays, we felt like we needed to address it first.) Our relationship with God influences every other aspect of our lives here on earth and forever determines how we'll spend eternity.

Soul care is placing our full trust in Jesus based on who He is and what He's done for us, and then choosing to follow Him (Luke 9:23; John 1:12). This is how real spiritual life begins.

After we've taken this important first step, we are on a lifelong journey to grow in Christ and know Him better. We grow much like a plant grows. In fact, on His last evening with His disciples, Jesus used a vivid analogy of a vine when He told them, "Abide in Me" (John 15:4, NKJV). Just as branches can't bear fruit unless they remain attached to the life-giving vine, we can't bear fruit unless we stay connected to Jesus. Abiding in Jesus is the most basic and essential way to nourish ourselves. This is ultimately how soul-care happens.

You might be thinking, *make it practical.* The truth is, with life running at such a rapid pace for most of us, we *must* intentionally nurture our relationship with God, spending time with Him to know Him better. I know this very well, because whenever I am not abiding deeply in Him—and I'm on my own—I get myself into trouble! Here are some practical ways you can nourish your soul:

• Set aside time each day to talk with God, praising and thanking Him, confessing your struggles and sin, and sharing your needs and concerns with Him.
• Read the Bible regularly, memorizing and meditating on Scripture.
• Genuinely seek to trust and obey God in every aspect of your life.
• Attend church regularly and become involved with other Christians who are pursuing God.
• Join a Bible study, prayer, or fellowship group—or a Wholehearted Wife group!

As you spend time with God and nurture your relationship with Him, you will begin to see growth in how you relate to others—not perfection, mind you, but growth. A heart under the Spirit's control is filled with love and grace toward others (Galatians 5:16–23.)

2. Caring for Your Heart

Interestingly, this second aspect of self-care is often the most difficult for us as women. When it comes to caring for our hearts, I (Erin) have talked with many who lack an understanding of really how to do this. And I can also attest through my own journey that I struggled with this greatly (and sometimes I still do).

Proverbs 4:23 warns us to "Above all else, guard your heart, for it is the wellspring of life." Maybe you're like me—left wondering how to do this. The heart is so integral to every aspect of our lives, we need to be especially careful to nourish and protect it. Although philosophers can debate what "the heart" actually is, one aspect of it is our emotional life. Think of emotions as God's information system. They inform us about our needs and deepest concerns. They also tend to drive our actions and reactions. This is why it's important to understand them rather than stuff them, deny them, or judge them. As we nourish our hearts and seek to understand our emotions, we can evaluate what they're telling us and consider how we'll respond.

Here are a few pointers to help you recognize, identify, and understand your emotions:

- *Pay attention to your emotions.* Instead of avoiding or denying them, ask yourself, "What am I feeling?" Often, emotions have a physiological manifestation. For example, fear and nervousness frequently express themselves as a sick feeling in the pit of your stomach or "butterflies." Try to identify what you're feeling without judging whether you should feel the way you do.

- *Think about the needs your feelings reveal and "name them."* When you've identified your feelings, consider what's at the root of them. In many instances, an unmet need or a disappointed expectation is hidden behind an emotion. Ask yourself, "What do I need from myself or from others? What is prompting these feelings?" And then take it one step further—name what you are feeling—not like you named your children, but put it into words. "I am feeling betrayed; unimportant; rejected."

• *Evaluate your feelings in light of truth.* Go to your loving heavenly Father and express your feelings to Him. Ask Him whether the feelings you identified reflect the truth. For example, let's say your girlfriend calls and says "I'm tired of you always cancelling our plans. You are so inconsiderate and unreliable!" You are left feeling many things, but let's go with "misportrayed" (name the feeling you are left with). As I ask my kids, "Just because they say it, does that make it true?" Go to Jesus and ask Him "Am I inconsiderate and unreliable? Help me to see myself from your perspective." I personally would rather live in the truth (John 8:32) and let Him be the source of that—not others. He may use your husband, your friends, or family members to help you become aware of your short-comings; however, He will follow that with conviction from the Holy Spirit. It may also be helpful to ask a godly person to help you evaluate your feelings in light of the truth in your particular situation.

There are many practical ways to care for yourself emotionally. For example, journaling what you are feeling after an experience or in order to express what you went through in a twenty-four-hour period (sometimes I'm in awe of all we do as women in one day!) can help you understand, express, and validate your feelings. If you find that you are stuck on an issue, talk to a trusted friend (we must have discernment about who these safe women are in our lives) or even a counselor. Looking back over the years, counseling has been very helpful to me during stressful times. There are also support groups or Celebrate Recovery groups that are topic-centered so you can learn from others who are dealing with similar struggles. There you will probably find great empathy, encouragement, practical suggestions, and books to read that can serve as their own mentors through specific issues.

Most of all, turn to God's Word for His infinite wisdom and encouragement. The psalms are filled with emotions that are honestly expressed to God. Ask God to help you recognize and manage your emotions.

Also, spend time thinking of things you enjoy that you can proactively do on a daily basis, almost like taking emotional vitamins. For me, walking outside (especially when it involves a girlfriend to talk to) does my heart good. Maybe it's running on the treadmill, sitting with a cup of tea, watching a good movie, reading a good book, listening to praise and worship music, or reading to your children. To be honest, I've been surprised by what nurtures my heart these days because of the uncanny similarity to my mother—a good cup of coffee and watching the birds out the window. I know, it doesn't sound super exciting, and I teased my mom about it for years. I'm guessing she's the one laughing now as I enjoy the simple beauty of birds and the warm flavor of a good cup of coffee. What is it for you?

3. Caring for Your Mind

The third aspect of self-care is nourishing our minds. The mind is a wonderful gift. With it we grow, learn, and expand our views of God and His amazing world.

What we spend our time thinking about has a great impact on our minds. This is why the apostle Paul wrote, "Whatever is true, whatever is noble, whatever is right, whatever is pure, whatever is lovely, whatever is admirable—if anything is excellent or praise worthy—think about such things" (Philippians 4:8). When we nourish our minds with what is right and true, we protect them from harmful influences and experience God's peace as a result (verse 7). Romans 8:6 says, "The mind of sinful man is death, but the mind controlled by the Spirit is life and peace." The mind is essentially a spiritual battleground between death and life, good and evil, truth and lies (Ephesians 6:12). This can be a difficult battle for many women. Satan loves to attack us through distorted thoughts.

So what can we ladies do to nourish our minds? There are many methods, some simple and some more involved. I can remember returning to graduate school at the age of thirty. After chasing toddlers all day long, I'd hit the classroom in the evenings. The environment of the classroom was a huge switch from my daytime hours, but it was enormously nourishing to me intellectually. However, there are other less complicated (and definitely cheaper) ways of nourishing your mind. Pick up a good book, listen to a podcast, read an article, watch an educational show, or exchange ideas with others. My favorite is to dig deeper into God's Word. (Bible Study Fellowship has certainly helped me do this.) Reading God's Word transforms us, renews us, and leads us into a deeper relationship with Jesus. Memorizing scripture keeps God's Word with us forever and gives our mind a great workout.

Recently, I received an email with a link to several sessions from a large women's conference. Watching each woman share from her heart caused me to reflect deeply. We can learn so much from each other either face-to-face or via the Internet. Really, we can serve as informal and formal mentors in each other's lives—challenging each other to think about life from different perspectives. Make sure that you seek wisdom from godly mentors and biblically sound websites or video sources. In 2 Timothy 3:14 Paul wrote to Timothy, "But as for you, continue in what you have learned and become convinced of, because you know those from whom you have learned it." In Philippians 4:9, Paul wrote, "Whatever you have learned or received or heard from me, or seen in me—put it into practice." Godly mentors—in person or via books and programs—can help show you how God's truth applies in your real-life situations.

4. Caring for Your Body

The fourth aspect of self-care relates to nourishing our bodies. The Bible tells believers that our bodies are temples of the Holy Spirit (1 Corinthians 6:19). God Himself lives in us and has given our bodies to us as temporary gifts to use for His glory. By taking good care of our bodies rather than neglecting, abusing, or misusing them, we're honoring God (verse 20). Sometimes it's easy to forget that our bodies ultimately belong to our Creator, not to us (verse 19). The truth is, caring for our bodies demonstrates our love and respect for God.

When we care for our bodies, we also show that we love ourselves. This is reflected in Ephesians 5:29 (NASB): "No one ever hated his own flesh, but nourishes and cherishes it."

Nourish to Flourish

- *Take time to rest.* Even Jesus recognized the importance of rest and renewal (Matthew 11:28–29; Mark 6:31).
- *Exercise regularly, at least three days a week.* The apostle Paul acknowledged that "physical training is of some value" (1 Timothy 4:8). So get out there and walk around your neighborhood or find other creative ways to move your body (e.g., join an exercise class, lift weights, dance, chop wood)!
- *Eat a balanced diet of healthy, nourishing food.* Avoid overeating or filling up on junk food that will ultimately harm your body. It's easy to turn to food during stressful times and become an emotional eater. Even though "everything is permissible . . . not everything is beneficial" (1 Corinthians 10:23–31). Remember that even

something as mundane as eating is a way to glorify
God (verse 31).

- *Get a good night's sleep.* Sleep is a gift (Psalm 127:2), as
  any sleep-deprived mom would agree. It's essential for
  functioning well in every area of life, so try to get at least
  seven hours a night.
- *Develop healthy habits.* Rather than swinging back and
  forth between extremes, be balanced. There's a lot of
  wisdom in the saying "All things in moderation."
- *Get regular physical exams.* Talk with your doctor about
  any health problems you're experiencing, even if they
  seem minor.

Weight is something that I have struggled with over the years. However, instead of ignoring the scale and how I feel physically, I continue to turn to the Lord to help me. I have found that consistent exercise, eating at home instead of out, and the assistance of a support group or even the accountability of a friend is helpful. Watching our weight is a battle worth fighting because it has an impact on how we feel.

When you love God with every part of your being, He fills you up to overflowing with His amazing love. Out of that overflow, you give to others. This is the balanced life, the only kind of life worth living. If you don't take care of yourself, you have no overflow. Without an overflow, you find it very hard to take care of others—and almost impossible to obey Jesus' command to love God wholeheartedly. If you and I want a healthy and satisfying life, all three pursuits must remain in balance: loving God and loving others with the same energy that we love ourselves.[1] When we seek to take care of ourselves—soul, heart, mind, and strength—we can respond to others out of a place of wholeness. As we abide in Christ, He becomes the source from which we ourselves are nourished and from which we can, in turn, nourish our husbands.

Nourishing Your Husband

As we discussed earlier, nourishing is the process of how we can help our spouses feel loved, cared for, and valued. Often the challenge is figuring out what "speaks" this to them personally—in essence, what actions really leave them feeling valued. I (Erin) can easily figure out what speaks love to me; however, when it comes to Greg, I have to dig a little deeper.

Encouragement requires empathy and seeing the world from your spouse's perspective. We must first learn what is important to our spouse. Only then can we give encouragement. With verbal encouragement, we are trying to communicate, "I know. I care. I am with you. How can I help?" We are trying to show that we believe in him and in his abilities. We are giving credit and praise.

—Gary Chapman, *The Five Love Languages: The Secret to Love that Lasts*

One way to think about giving to my husband is a banking concept. In a shared account, both Greg and I make deposits and withdrawals regularly. Being the more forgetful one with recording these actions, I've learned that I can go online and check the activity of the account and quickly see where we're at. The same is true in balancing our marital bank accounts. If we don't really know what qualifies as a withdrawal (debit) or a credit in our husbands' emotional bank accounts, we need to find out.

Think about it: your husband has had a different upbringing, a different family, and many different life experiences that all shape what speaks love to him. However, the great news is that it really isn't hard to discover simple actions you can take to make large deposits in his emotional bank account. First, have him complete the following sentence "I feel loved when you . . ." We regularly have couples do this at our seminars and it's always amazing to me to hear the variety of responses. Just this weekend, one husband shared that he feels loved when his wife throws his bath towel into the dryer while he's in the shower and then greets him with a warm towel when he's ready to get out. Wow! I know that I couldn't do that every time Greg showers, but every now and then—what a treat! (I actually added that to my list! But this section isn't about me!)

Over the years, Greg and I regularly pull out our "I feel loved when you . . ." lists while we are on long road trips. We add to it as we discover new and exciting ways that we can best speak love to one another through our actions. However, if your husband is unwilling to do this or is having a difficult time identifying what would top his list, simply spend time observing what matters to him. Try different approaches (thinking through different love languages) and see what he responds to. Is it quality time while doing something together or a back massage before bed? Keep a running list and continually add to it.

I've learned a new way of nourishing Greg since moving to Colorado. You see, since we moved, Greg has worked tirelessly writing several books and hosting a daily call-in radio program on top of his full-time duties. By about the third month, I could see exhaustion written all over his face. Finally, he decided to take a much needed day off of work to rest. In my mind, I expected him to stay in his pajamas all day and watch movies. (Since he is more introverted, I thought this would be rejuvenating for him.) However, I was stunned when he announced that he wanted to get up super early and drive up to the mountains and fish all day. Honestly, this surprised me because when I'm exhausted, the last thing I'd want to do is get up early, jump into the car, drive two hours and then stand in the sun holding a pole. I couldn't imagine that Greg would return refreshed and recharged. However, around 4:00 p.m., I heard the garage door open and Greg came in smiling, laughing, and, yes, rejuvenated. He told me all about the beauty of the river, the fish he'd caught and released, the alone time in the car, and just how good it was for him to have the adventure of the day. He finished by telling me how loved he felt because I encouraged him to go, and he thanked me profusely for helping make it happen. Then he said, "Next time, I'd like you to come with me!" And in fact I did. Although the day was not my perfect day, and frankly I felt exhausted from getting up so early, I know that it made him feel loved, honored and valued. It left him feeling nourished, and that was my goal.

Although you might define a deposit very differently than your husband, you need to continue to strive to understand him. Continue asking questions and observing to gain a greater understanding of what truly communicates love and honor to your man.

The following list describes some common deposits for husbands. This list may be helpful in identifying relational needs in your marriage, but remember one important thing: There is no substitute for knowing and understanding your unique, God-designed spouse.

Use this list as a starting point to fill your husband's emotional bank account while you learn what is uniquely important to him:

- Value his opinions and advice
- Cheer his successes and encourage him when he fails
- Praise his strengths and show grace toward his weaknesses
- Forgive him when he hurts you

- Express delight in him and make him the object of your undivided attention when you're together (without the kids)
- Listen to him and take a genuine interest in him
- Focus on his positive qualities rather than his negative qualities
- Speak of him to others with sincere love and affection
- Demonstrate that you trust him
- Express thanks for his help
- Choose to believe the best about him and give him the benefit of the doubt
- Protect your time together
- Speak to him with grace-filled words
- Be loyal to him and stand by him when life is hard
- Tell him that you not only love him, but that you also genuinely like him.

Ladies, I (Erin) know that we are all busy caring for others. And often it's easy to set our husbands aside so we can focus on our children or others. However, our husbands have needs that only we can meet. We want them to feel nourished—especially by us.

Nourishing Your Marriage

As we learned earlier, the dictionary defines *nourish* as "[providing] food or other substances necessary for life and growth." When we nourish our husbands, we're also nourishing our marriages—providing what's necessary for the life and growth of our relationships as husbands and wives.

It seems as if nourishing our marriages should come naturally, like nourishing our bodies with nutritious food. Yet many marriages are malnourished. One of the main culprits is busyness. Dr. James Dobson and many other marriage specialists have pointed out that in today's rat-race world, overcommitment and exhaustion are pervasive marriage killers.

It almost goes without saying that life can be stressful and demanding. As couples, we get so caught up in our careers, children, and obligations that our days may feel like a series of tasks and events to cross off our to-do lists. By the time evening arrives, both of us are often worn out and in need of some alone time. Obviously this hinders our ability to enjoy each other and our marriage.

We often get so busy doing life that we forget that spending enjoyable time together is as important as discussing our frustrations and hurts, paying our bills, and getting the household chores done. In fact, without the ability to have fun time together, our marriages and time together become synonymous with what feels like a business meeting. Really, what it boils down to is becoming proactive in nourishing your marriage. And honestly, this isn't that hard. We have found inserting three things into your marriage can be life giving.

First, make sure that every day you have a daily connection. During this time, set all "administrating" aside—don't talk about the kids, the finances, or the in-laws. Simply connect. Connect like you did when you were dating or courting. Ask questions, share what has happened throughout your day, and check in on each other's heart. Secondly, have a regular date night. Again, set the business meeting aside and go out and do something fun together. Something new and exciting is even better, but most important, just enjoy each other. Escape from your daily duties and enjoy a night out together. (Setting aside a date night weekly would be ideal, but at least get out monthly together even if it is something simple like a special dessert and activity after the kids are in bed.) And third, plan for a yearly adventure. For many this may come in the form of a vacation or a weekend away. However, it doesn't need to be expensive or elaborate. You could go for a long drive out of town, attend a marriage retreat, go camping, or do a weekend "staycation" while grandparents or friends watch the kids. Or if you have the funds and the babysitting—head to Hawaii. Whatever it is for you, plan this together and, again, simply enjoy the time away refreshing, renewing and nourishing your marriage.

Keeping these three components in mind, we are going to bring this section to a close by offering some simple ways to nourish your marriage amidst the chaos and busyness. Use these as a starting point to think of how you can best nourish your marriage in the simplest of ways.

Dream about what God might be calling the two of you together to do as a couple—is it a mission trip, opening a business together, teaching a class at church, or adopting a child?

Pray for each other—not just at meals, but as a regular, specifically focused commitment. What are specific things he's dealing with that you can pray for? Maybe stress at work? A struggle he faces regularly? An area that God is growing him in?

Play a game together or go to the park and shoot baskets.

Brainstorm new things you'd both like to try (rock climbing, horseback riding, cooking classes) and then follow through and do it!

Record a show or series you both are interested in and watch it together on a weekly basis or read a book together and talk about it.

Spend time going for walks and share what God has been teaching you.

Do something to nurture your marriage every year—attend a marriage weekend retreat, read a marriage book, or host a marriage small group in your home

Don't just attend church; volunteer to serve together at church.

Develop questions that you can ask each other at least once a week to take the conversation to a heart level.

Leave each other love notes.

Take time to show a sign of affection when one of you leaves the home in the morning or comes home at the end of the day.

The bottom line is this: Your marriage doesn't have a cruise-control switch you can engage in hopes that everything will be fine as you glide on down the road together. You must decide to invest every day in your marriage and ask yourself, "What will I do to nourish my marriage today?"

><><><><><><><><><><><><><><   ♥ ♥ ♥   ><><><><><><><><><><><><><><

True love is not a feeling. . . . It is the
choice to invest time, energy, and
money to accomplish that goal.

—Gary Chapman, *Happily Ever After*

><><><><><><><><><><><><><><   ♥ ♥ ♥   ><><><><><><><><><><><><><><

We all long to have more loving relationships with our spouses, but it won't just magically happen. First, we must be well cared for—our souls, our hearts, our minds, and our bodies. Only then can we can love and serve our husbands from a place of fullness. When we are consistently empty, drained, and worn out—we cannot love wholeheartedly. As we abide in Christ, we can truly love and nourish our husbands and our marriage relationships.

Key Three: Accepting Personality and Other Differences

◇◇◇◇◇◇◇◇◇◇◇◇◇◇◇◇ ♥ ♥ ♥ ◇◇◇◇◇◇◇◇◇◇◇◇◇◇◇◇

Understanding Our Unique Design

Do you ever wonder why your husband does what he does? For that matter, maybe you're not even sure why you do what you do! Perhaps you've never given much thought to understanding your husband, much less yourself. Or maybe you're well aware of your own personality but aren't so sure about your husband's.

What first attracts us to our spouses is often a personality quality we admire or find exciting. We may even find ourselves drawn to a quality that differs significantly from the way we're designed. In many cases, opposites really do attract.

But as I (Erin) mentioned earlier, after Greg and I married, I discovered that we had a hard time seeing eye to eye because we were so different. We had different personalities, different habits, different likes and dislikes. We did laundry differently, spent our free time differently, and had differing opinions. Differences that never seemed to be an obstacle when we were dating suddenly drove a wedge between us and pushed us to the brink of separation. The differences in our personalities that once attracted us to each other began to irritate and confuse us.

Whether you and your husband clash like plaids and polka dots or are cut out of the same cloth, no marriage is blissfully free of irritation or conflict over personality differences. Having the grace to accept personality differences in your marriage is vital to a more loving relationship.

But how can we, as wholehearted wives, learn to accept these differences if we have only a vague or incomplete understanding of our husbands' personalities, or our own?

Encarta Dictionary, defines *personality* as "the totality of somebody's attitudes, interests, behavioral patterns, emotional responses, social roles, and other individual traits that endure over long periods of time." That definition alone tells us that personality isn't a simplistic notion. God designed each of us with amazing intricacy. We truly are "fearfully and wonderfully made" (Psalm 139:14)! But in all of our complexity, it's no wonder we find it difficult to understand our spouses and ourselves.

In this chapter we'll explore the concept of personality, learn more about ourselves and our spouses, and discuss ways to bridge the gap between our differences. Understanding both your husband's personality and your own will give you a deeper appreciation for who God has uniquely created you both to be, even when your husband's behavior confuses or irritates you.

Understanding Yourself

Until I was in college, I (Erin) had no idea of the value of understanding my own personality. Actually, I couldn't have described my personality if you'd asked me. I hadn't ever stopped to reflect on my attitudes, typical emotions, or behavior patterns—even though they were certainly part of me. But as a college sophomore at Grand Canyon University, I had the chance to gain some insight into my personality strengths and weaknesses.

I began dating Greg's roommate that year and, ironically, soon discovered that Greg's sister, Kari, had dated him the previous year. Kari was quite curious about this new girl who was dating her ex-boyfriend, so she began reaching out to me. We had many lunch dates over teriyaki chicken and California rolls and quickly discovered that we actually enjoyed each other.

Over lunch one day, Kari suggested I take a personality test that her dad was using in his speaking and counseling ministry. I had never heard of such a test, but this new friend seemed to have my best interests at heart, so I decided to take her advice and learn more about my personality.

Later that afternoon Kari showed up at my apartment with the test and told me to stay in my bedroom until I completed it. After I finished, Kari tallied up the results and proudly announced that I was a combination of an Otter and a Golden Retriever. Was this some cruel joke? Was Kari really calling me a small, aquatic animal with some dog thrown in? But as she began to describe the Otter and the Golden Retriever personalities to me, I felt years of questioning melt away. You see, I was adopted as an infant and often felt that I was somehow wired very differently from others in my family. While I couldn't put my finger on it, I had actually arrived at the conclusion that there was something wrong with me.

Now, after years of doubting myself, I suddenly had an explanation for why I was the way I was. There wasn't anything wrong with me; I simply had a different personality than my mom or dad. When Kari explained that this was how God made me, utter relief flowed through me. It was really a life-changing moment.

When you understand your own personality, you gain insight into your strengths and growth areas. You also learn what a balanced life looks like for you individually and in your marriage.

I'd like to encourage you to take the following assessment to better understand your own personality.[1] You'll be surprised at how much you'll learn about yourself in a few short minutes. As you'll see, everyone generally exhibits some characteristics from each of the personality types, but one or two dominating traits usually characterize behavior.

Keep in mind that *this is not an all-or-nothing inventory.* Behavior can't always be neatly categorized and labeled. But giving some thought to how we typically act, respond, and feel allows us to gain understanding into ourselves and our spouses. The assessment also gives us word pictures and vocabulary to use to more easily discuss the complicated aspects of personality.

<><><><><><><><><><><><><><><><><><><><><><><><><><><><><><><><><><><><>

Discover Your Personality Profile

Beginning with column 1, work your way through each section, marking your responses in the spaces provided. Use the following scale to identify the degree to which each characteristic or behavior most accurately describes how you relate to your loved ones.

0 = not at all / 1 = somewhat / 2 = mostly / 3 = very much

I	II	III	IV
__ Likes control	__ Enthusiastic	__ Sensitive	__ Consistent
__ Confident	__ Visionary	__ Calm	__ Reserved
__ Firm	__ Energetic	__ Non-demanding	__ Practical
__ Likes challenge	__ Promoter	__ Enjoys routine	__ Factual
__ Problem solver	__ Moves easily	__ Relational	__ Perfectionistic
__ Bold	__ Fun-loving	__ Adaptable	__ Detailed
__ Goal driven	__ Spontaneous	__ Thoughtful	__ Inquisitive
__ Strong-willed	__ Likes new ideas	__ Patient	__ Persistent
__ Self-reliant	__ Optimistic	__ Good listener	__ Sensitive
__ Persistent	__ Takes risks	__ Loyal	__ Accurate
__ Takes charge	__ Motivator	__ Even-keeled	__ Controlled
__ Determined	__ Very verbal	__ Gives in	__ Predictable
__ Enterprising	__ Friendly	__ Indecisive	__ Orderly
__ Competitive	__ Popular	__ Dislikes change	__ Conscientious

I	II	III	IV
__ Productive	__ Enjoys variety	__ Dry humor	__ Discerning
__ Purposeful	__ Group oriented	__ Sympathetic	__ Analytical
__ Adventurous	__ Initiator	__ Nurturing	__ Precise
__ Independent	__ Inspirational	__ Tolerant	__ Scheduled
__ Action oriented	__ Likes change	__ Peacemaker	__ Deliberate
__ **Total**	__ **Total**	__ **Total**	__ **Total**

Now add up the total in each column. The highest score indicates your dominant personality type.

Discover the Value of Your Personality

	Lion	Otter	Golden Retriever	Beaver
Relational Strengths	Takes charge	Optimistic Energetic	Warm and relational	Accurate and precise
	Problem solver			
	Competitive	Motivator	Loyal	Quality control
	Enjoys change	Future oriented	Enjoys routine	Discerning
	Confrontational		Peacemaker	Analytical
			Sensitive feelings	

	Lion	Otter	Golden Retriever	Beaver
Strengths Out of Balance	Too direct or impatient	Unrealistic or daydreamer	Attracts the hurting	Too critical or too strict
	Too busy	Impatient or overbearing	Missed opportunities	Too controlling
	Cold-blooded			Too negative toward new opportunities
	Impulsive or takes big risks	Manipulator or pushy	Stays in a rut	
		Avoids details or lacks follow-through	Sacrifices own feelings for harmony	Loses overview
	Insensitive to others		Easily hurt or holds a grudge	

	Lion	Otter	Golden Retriever	Beaver
Communication Style	Direct or blunt One-way *Weakness*: Not as good a listener	Can inspire others Optimistic or enthusiastic One-way *Weakness*: High energy can manipulate others	Indirect Two-way Great listener *Weakness*: Uses too many words or provides too many details	Factual Two-way Great listener *Weakness*: Desire for detail and precision can frustrate others

	Lion	Otter	Golden Retriever	Beaver
Relational Needs	Personal attention and recognition for what they do Areas where he or she can be in charge Opportunity to solve problems Freedom to change Challenging activities	Approval Opportunity to verbalize Visibility Social recognition	Emotional security Agreeable environment	Quality Exact expectations

	Lion	Otter	Golden Retriever	Beaver
Relational Balance	Add softness Become a great listener	Be attentive to spouse's needs There is such a thing as too much optimism	Learn to say no; establish emotional boundaries Learn to confront when own feelings are hurt	Total support is not always possible Thorough explanation isn't everything

As you completed this short assessment, I'm hoping that you had some moments of understanding yourself a little bit better. You may have already had a general understanding of your personality. However, it's always helpful to revisit your temperament strengths and weaknesses and keep in mind how you were "knit together."

The Benefits of Understanding Your Personality

As I (Erin) mentioned earlier, understanding my personality profile set me free from a lot of turmoil and confusion about myself. What a relief it was to find out that I was simply different from my family members—and that these differences were okay, even good and God designed. Understanding my personality helped me accept myself and become more aware of my strengths and growth areas. Knowing how God designed me has also enabled me to enhance my strengths and work on my growth areas.

Let's look at some of the benefits of understanding our personalities.

Balancing Your Strengths and Growth Areas

Understanding ourselves enables us to recognize more quickly when a personality trait is getting out of balance. Most of us are painfully aware of the times our weaknesses (growth areas) become unbalanced, but how can our strengths get out of balance?

Balancing Your Response to Stress

Stress can often cause us to function in an out-of-balance mode, and as wives and moms, we don't seem to be lacking in the stress department. As a matter of fact, a new study just released from The Barna Group (*www.Barna.org*) found that 72 percent of married women report feeling stressed out.[2] The more pressure we feel, the more we look for a coping mechanism. And that coping mechanism can often be tied to a personality strength—something that feels comfortable, soothing, or refreshing.

When we understand our personalities and how we tend to cope with stress, we can take steps to deal with it in healthier ways. Some of us turn to comfort food when we're stressed, but often our cravings for comfort are cloaking a need for connection with people. I (Erin) tend to cope with stress by becoming more extroverted and social. But knowing that this trait can swing to an extreme under stress helps me seek out connection without driving my introverted husband crazy.

◇◇◇◇◇◇◇◇◇◇◇◇◇◇◇◇◇◇◇◇◇◇◇ ♥♥♥ ◇◇◇◇◇◇◇◇◇◇◇◇◇◇◇◇◇◇◇◇◇◇◇

Without exception, our weaknesses are simply a reflection of our personality strengths being pushed to an extreme.

—Dr. John Trent

◇◇◇◇◇◇◇◇◇◇◇◇◇◇◇◇◇◇◇◇◇◇◇ ♥♥♥ ◇◇◇◇◇◇◇◇◇◇◇◇◇◇◇◇◇◇◇◇◇◇◇

By understanding ourselves better, we can recognize when a personality trait is swinging to an extreme under stress. One of the first steps in dealing with an out-of-balance stress response is noticing when it's happening. The best thing we can do for ourselves and our loved ones is to recognize the warning signs and deal with stress in healthier, more balanced ways.

Accepting Yourself the Way God Does

Two of the biggest lies the Evil One whispers in our ears are "You aren't good enough" and "You don't really matter." Our culture echoes those lies, bombarding us with messages that tell us we're not smart enough, beautiful enough, talented enough, good enough—you name it. Even our personalities don't seem to measure up. We think we need to be more and do more to be acceptable to others, including God. No wonder we have such a hard time accepting ourselves!

My (Erin's) daughter Taylor posted this on Facebook a few months into her freshman year of college:

This past month and a half, I have constantly been learning that I am simply not good enough. I am not smart enough, pretty enough, strong enough, etc. But I've also been learning that the beauty of grace is found in this: I have *never* nor will I *ever* be called to do or be *any* of these things. All I will ever be called to do is love God, love others, and love myself enough to let go of my expectations and standards and allow *Him* to take care of the rest. I'm incredibly thankful to be learning to find all of my hope, joy, love and strength in these truths instead of in myself or in this world. My God is so good.

When I saw her post, my first thought was, *I wish I'd "got it" like that when I was eighteen years old.* And my second thought was, *I hope I'll grasp it at forty-four years of age!*

The insight I've gained into my own personality over the years has been a significant step of growth in my life! Understanding myself has cleared away the confusion and self-doubt I felt for so long and has enabled me to begin accepting myself the way God does.

I can't encourage you enough to understand the way God designed you and to embrace your strengths and growth areas. Sin makes us all unworthy, but God has declared you worthy in Jesus Christ. Accept yourself as a person of unique value to God simply because He created you and loves you.[3] You are a complete package—imperfect but beautiful!

Understanding Your Husband

Have you ever met a woman who entered marriage hoping that her husband would never change? Maybe a few of them exist out there somewhere, but it seems that the majority of us hope we can smooth a few of our husbands' rough edges after the wedding. Let's be honest. We think, *A little tweak here and there surely couldn't hurt anyone.* When we marry, the personality traits we adored when we were dating sometimes become as irritating as the sound of fingernails scratching on a chalkboard. We determine that our husbands need a little work to become, well . . . more like us! We may not realize that's our agenda, but all too often it is. After all, what's not to like about our personalities? Why wouldn't our husbands want to add a few of our finer qualities to their personality profile?

When we're dating, we're often attracted to the qualities that make our future husbands different from us. Even if a couple has shared values and similar interests, gender traits and temperament differences make the other person seem fascinating. These differences make a relationship more exciting and conversations more stimulating. We eagerly soak up new details about each other. We relish the nuances and explore the vast depths of our interests and experiences as if we're digging for buried treasure.

As the popular adage goes, "Variety is the spice of life." The more variety, the better . . . when we're dating, that is. But after we marry, differences can suddenly become sources of frustration and conflict. The appreciation we may once have felt for our spouses' unique qualities may give way to confusion, irritation, and criticism. Love may be overshadowed by anger. Disrespect may replace honor. Control may destroy freedom. We may wonder what happened to the men we married. When we fell in love, they seemed perfect. When we married, they needed only a little tweaking here and there. But as our differences begin to wear thin, we may conclude that our husbands need a complete overhaul!

Wanting to change our husbands after we marry may result from the realization that marriage isn't the dream life we thought it would be. We may not have anticipated that our personality differences would rub us the wrong way or drive us to criticize, nag, and argue. Perhaps we never envisioned that marriage would give us such a strong dose of reality.

The antidote to our disillusionment is seeking to understand our husbands' personalities better. We need to renew our appreciation for the qualities we valued when we were first getting to know each other. We need to view our spouses as treasured gifts. Accepting and valuing our personality differences are important keys to more loving relationships with our spouses and ultimately becoming more wholehearted wives.

With that in mind, let's explore the benefits of understanding our husbands' personalities:

1. Loving our husbands more fully and compassionately. How can understanding your husband's personality help you love him more fully? The truth is, gaining greater insight into how God made your husband should soften your heart toward him and help you view him with more compassion. During stressful times in your marriage, understanding why he does what he does can help you walk through conflicts with grace and forgiveness.

It can be tempting to use our knowledge about our husbands as ammunition against them. But rather than fueling criticism and rejection, understanding their personalities should strengthen our love for them. Remember, even though God knows everything about you (Psalm 139), good and bad, His love for you is filled with grace and compassion (Psalm 103:8–18). Ask God to help you see your husband through His eyes of love as you seek to understand him better.

2. Knowing our husbands more intimately. A number of years ago, I (Greg) learned an interesting mnemonic device—one of those little words or sayings that helps you remember facts or, in my case, the meaning of a word. When you say the word *intimacy* slowly, it sounds a little like "into-me-see." Isn't that a great way to think of the meaning of the word?

Intimacy has to do with seeing deeply into another person, knowing him or her at more than just a surface level. God has placed within each of us the longing to be deeply known. God Himself knows everything about us (Psalm 139:1). He knew us before we were conceived in the womb, and He is familiar with all our ways (Jeremiah 1:4–5; Psalm 139:3).

As Erin's husband, I want her to know and understand me intimately. In the blockbuster movie *Avatar*, the alien Na'vi people would greet one another by saying, "I see you." That's what I want in our marriage—for Erin to see me. That means looking past the superficial masks I may wear and the behaviors that frustrate her and seeing the real me.

One of the best ways to know your husband more intimately is asking him to take the personality assessment presented earlier in the chapter. Make sure to tell him that this will allow you to better understand his strengths and meet his needs. If Erin said something like this to me, I'd take a personality inventory anytime! However, if your husband is deeply opposed to taking the assessment or you don't feel you can approach him about it at this point in your relationship, then don't. Instead, spend some time reflecting on the inventory, thinking about the characteristics or words that best describe him. Although the results will reflect your perceptions of his personality rather than his, it's a starting point that will help you understand him more deeply.

If your husband agrees to take the assessment and is open to sharing the results with you, offer to share yours with him as well. By gaining insight and understanding into how God designed your husband, you'll come to know him more intimately as a person, and you'll deepen the intimacy in your relationship.

3. *Seeing our husbands' value.* I (Greg) know that at times my Golden Retriever personality frustrates my wife. There are plenty of

times when, as an introvert, I avoid being around other people and would rather just be alone. I also have a pretty laid-back attitude that says, "Whatever"—which basically means "Who cares about the details?"

I'm not a big risk taker, and I like routine. In fact, I would much rather stay at home than go out. I like watching television and playing video games with the kids. And yet in spite of all my preferences and quirks, somehow, someway Erin sees my value. She's like the person William Arthur Ward described when he said, "A true friend knows your weaknesses but shows you your strengths; feels your fears but fortifies your faith; sees your anxieties but frees your spirit; recognizes your disabilities but emphasizes your possibilities."

4. Recognizing our husbands' strengths. It's human nature to focus on weaknesses rather than strengths and to complain about what's wrong with others instead of what's right. As a wife and a friend and a counselor, I (Erin) see that sometimes we women all too often squelch our husbands' growth by nitpicking at their flaws and failings. The book of Proverbs says that living on the "corner of a roof" or in a desert is better than living with a "quarrelsome wife" (Proverbs 21:9, 19). When we focus on our husbands' weaknesses, we miss out on the opportunity to encourage them to excel at their strengths.

Author and pastor Chuck Swindoll shared a story he once read that illustrates the importance of recognizing our husbands' God-given strengths and encouraging them to use those natural strengths and abilities to their fullest potential.

It seems that some animals started a school and decided to take the same courses. The curriculum included flying, swimming, climbing, and running. The duck excelled at swimming, the rabbit at running, the squirrel at climbing, and the eagle at flying. But when the duck tried to improve its running skills, its webbed feet were ruined for swimming. After that, the duck was only an average swimmer. Likewise, the rabbit got a twitch in its leg from swimming and couldn't run as fast after that. The squirrel developed a charley horse from trying to fly, which ruined its stellar grade in climbing. And the eagle flunked climbing because it insisted on flying to the top of the tree. (The eagle was a nonconformist.)

Swindoll concluded,

> A duck is a duck—and *only* a duck. It is built to swim, not
> to run or fly and certainly not to climb. A squirrel is a squir-
> rel—and *only* that. To move it out of its forte, climbing, and
> then expect it to swim or fly will drive a squirrel nuts. Eagles are
> beautiful creatures in the air but not in a foot race. The rabbit
> will win every time unless, of course, the eagle gets hungry.
>
> What is true of creatures in the forest is true of Christians
> in the family. . . . God has not made us all the same. He never
> intended to. It was He who planned and designed [our] differ-
> ences, unique capabilities, and variations. . . .
>
> So relax. . . . Appreciate the members of your family . . . for
> who they are, even though their outlook or style may be miles
> different from yours. Rabbits don't fly. Eagles don't swim. Ducks
> look funny trying to climb. Squirrels don't have feathers.[4]

So if your husband is an eagle, don't expect him to swim. Affirm his ability to soar! If he's a duck, let him glide through the water rather than forcing him to climb a tree just because it comes naturally to you. Seek to understand how he's built so that you can recognize his strengths and encourage him to excel at them.

5. *Responding with more grace to their stress.* As Erin mentioned earlier, all of us can get out of balance and end up functioning in the extremes of our personalities. Perhaps this occurs most often when we feel stress. Most men I (Greg) know have a great desire to be successful.

And most experience a certain amount of stress from the demands of their jobs.

Research shows that men deal with stress differently than women do. As a man's stress level increases, his body produces more oxytocin hormone, which is further influenced by testosterone. These chemicals trigger a fight-or-flight response. In other words, when stressed, men either act more aggressively or withdraw (we like to say "go into their cave").

Women also produce more oxytocin, but it's coupled with estrogen and has a different result: When stressed, women tend to lean into relationships, either protectively nurturing their children or seeking out other female friends. Researchers have called this the "tend-and-befriend" response.[5]

Basically, these chemical reactions set men and women up to respond very differently during times of stress—the perfect combination for conflict. Women want to connect, and men feel more ready to pick a fight or withdraw. Maybe this explains why some men want to read the paper, watch television, or be alone for a few minutes when they come home after a stressful day at work. Just a word of caution— sometimes gender differences can seem pretty stereotypical. We must remember that this scenario may look different in your marriage—but researchers have found this to occur in many relationships.

As much as I would like to avoid being on edge or wish I didn't feel the desire to isolate when I pull in the driveway after a hard day, it really does help when Erin gives me an understanding look and allows me a chance to unwind before dinner or a deep discussion. I can't tell you how much it means to me as a man when Erin comes alongside me with understanding and encouragement rather than criticism. It changes my whole outlook!

How you respond to your husband when he's under stress has a direct impact on his behavior toward you. I (Erin) can remember when Greg was in graduate school. He was under enormous pressure. During this season, I gave him extra space to retreat when he needed to and we also agreed that he needed healthy outlets for his stress. So, he began training for a marathon. Yes, this required more time away from Taylor and me; however, I knew that overall we were benefitting from this activity. He was able to engage with us more fully after having an outlet to deal with the stress level.

As we continue to understand how our husbands are different, it will allow us to love them more fully. For me, understanding Greg's differences has helped me to stop judging him and start embracing him. I hope this is also the case for you. Ultimately, however, differences will also impact our marriage relationships.

Personality Differences in Your Marriage

Now that we've looked at understanding our own personalities as well as our spouses', let's look at how this idea of personality relates to our marriage relationships. The truth is that all marriages look different because they're made up of two unique individuals who are joined to become one. Every marriage combines gender differences, two distinct personalities, and a unique blend of strengths and weaknesses.

Recently I (Erin) witnessed a beautiful illustration of this idea of two individuals blending together to make a unique marriage. Some dear friends were celebrating their twenty-fifth wedding anniversary, and they wanted to commemorate the milestone by renewing their wedding vows with all of their friends and family present. Ed and Renee invited several hundred people to join them in their Colorado Springs backyard—a breathtaking scene against the foothills of Pikes Peak. Rain had drizzled earlier in the day, but the sun broke through just in time for the ceremony—and along with it appeared a rainbow, almost as if it were a sign from above. What most guests didn't know was that Ed had been diagnosed with cancer earlier that week.

This amazing couple was facing an uncertain future but wanted to celebrate the rich twenty-five years they had shared. Those years hadn't all been easy. Neither of them were followers of Christ when they married, and they readily went along with the world's ways. Then over a period of months, each of them independently entered a relationship with Jesus. This changed everything. Their decisions to commit themselves to the Lord transformed not only each of them individually but it also transformed their marriage. Who they were as a couple, where they put their money, the ministry desires they shared, how they ran their business, what they did in their parenting—the list could go on and on; everything changed when they decided to serve Jesus. So on this very special day of remembering all God had done in and through their marriage, they signified their union with a sand unity candle.

Ed and Renee had purchased a clear glass vase, and each of them had their own vial of colored sand. Ed has an easy-going personality and chose blue sand to represent himself. Renee chose a bright pink sand, since her personality is a little more spicy and outgoing. As they simultaneously poured their vials of pink and blue sand into the vase, it became a beautiful representation of their uniqueness as a couple. This vase of mixed sand illustrated so perfectly how the blending of two distinct individuals—male and female both with different personalities—forms its own unique composite. Marriage truly is a beautiful piece of art that the Holy One creates when He joins two together as one.

Dealing with Differences in Marriage

The differences in our marriage are not always my (Erin) favorite thing to address in our marriage. I don't wake up thinking, *Wow, I can't wait to chat with Greg about our differences that we have dealt with over the past week.* Often, these conversations can be difficult due to buttons getting pushed and reactions setting off, many times resulting in conflict.

Sometimes, my feelings just simply get hurt when Greg helps me become aware of how one of my traits is impacting him. Often, it's one of my strengths out of balance. Our hope, however, is that we can view our differences as gifts to bring balance into our marriage relationship. Then the conversations might not be so dreaded.

I remember the day Greg took me aside and told me how exhausting it was for him to reach the weekend after working all week, only to discover that I had made social plans for both of us on Friday and Saturday nights—and sometimes on Sunday evenings as well. I immediately took great offense to his comment and thought, *What's wrong with him? Having friends is fun, and the only time we can get together is on the weekends.*

I bit my lip and listened as he proposed that we limit our social events to one night each weekend and spend the other nights alone as a couple. Again, I didn't understand how he could want that. I could have made social plans every single moment of the weekend, eating each meal with a friend or another couple.

But as Greg continued to share, a light bulb went off in my head. My personality as a strong Otter was much more social than his more introverted and slower-paced temperament as a Golden Retriever. After a demanding week of work, he needed some quiet and a little downtime. As I gave it more thought and prayed about it, I realized that my extroverted Otter mode had been out of balance. And I definitely hadn't stopped to consider my husband's needs and personality. Understanding my own temperament helped me realize that I needed to tone down my inner Otter. What I perceived as one of my greatest strengths became an obstacle in my relationship with Greg.

When you brush up against differences in your marriage (whether it's a personality difference or a gender difference), follow these tips to deal with them in a manner that will give you best results:

1. Reduce our tendency to "fix" our husbands. Ruth Bell Graham once remarked, "It's my job to love and respect Billy. It's God's job to make him good." When most of us see a problem, our first inclination is often to fix it. But in our marriage relationship that isn't usually the best course of action. My (Greg's) advice is this: Whatever you do, don't try to fix your husband, even when his flaws and personality differences irritate you. The more you try, the more he'll shut down and retreat—which ultimately leaves the overall environment in the marriage feeling really unsafe. Speaking from experience, when Erin has tried to fix me, it has led to nothing more than resistance on my part, and it often lands us in an argument.

Let me share a personal example of difference in habits between us. For some reason I have a unique style of holding my eating utensils. I actually had no idea this was the case until Erin informed me. At dinner one night, she suggested that I try holding my fork in a different manner.

Why does she have to change everything? I thought. *I've been eating this way my whole life, and it's been just fine.*

I realize now that she was just trying to help me with proper etiquette, but initially it felt like control and manipulation. It was just one of those things that felt critical upon delivery. And her timing didn't help. Bringing up the issue right when she noticed it probably seemed like a good idea to her. But it was the last thing I wanted to have analyzed at dinnertime, especially when I was supposed to be enjoying the food and my family. So when she offered her advice, the rest of the meal became very quiet.

May I suggest that minor irritations (and perhaps even major ones) are best brought up after the fact rather than in the heat of the moment when emotions may be running high. And sometimes it's better to overlook little behavioral quirks if they're not causing a major problem in your marriage relationship.

Whenever we try to fix someone, we're demonstrating a lack of acceptance. Understanding the unique way God designed your husband can help you focus on loving him and accepting his personality and behavioral quirks rather than trying to fix him. When he truly does need correction, use grace-filled words and remember that it's God's job to make him good. Although it takes two to create a "safe-haven" marriage, you certainly can influence the over-all temperature of your relationship by approaching him with grace.

2. Avoid negativity. If you find that you're able to notice only negative things about your spouse, marriage, or anyone for that matter, you can be almost 99.9 percent sure that you're under the influence—the influence of negative beliefs, that is. When all you can see are the weaknesses of your husband's personality, you are heading down the damaging pathway of negative beliefs.

In an earlier chapter, I (Greg) mentioned this tendency, which psychologists call "confirmation bias." It basically means that whatever you're looking for in someone's behavior (your bias) is exactly what you'll notice (your confirmation). In essence, that person is powerless against your beliefs because—you guessed it—he or she can't control you or your thoughts.

You must fight these nasty beliefs in any relationship, but especially in your marriage. You can do this best by adopting an "I could be wrong" attitude and giving your husband the benefit of the doubt. Basically this means having a perspective that leaves room for the possibility that you've misinterpreted some irritating behavior you notice in your spouse. Giving your husband the gift of believing the best about him and his intentions conquers negativity. In most instances I think we men rarely try to intentionally hurt our wives. But sometimes we do things without much thought of how it will impact you.

3. Allow room for both of you in your marriage. As we have said, you and your husband probably have discovered many differences. Part of having a healthy marriage relationship involves allowing room for both of you—quirks and all. If there is something that is annoying to you, check your heart first. Is it something that needs to be addressed or is it simply your preference? The wholehearted wife looks first within.

See the Ways You're Great Together

Your marriage is made up of both strengths and growth areas, especially because of the personality differences you each bring to the union. Notice we call them "growth areas," because that's just what they are— not weaknesses but opportunities for growth. Typically, as humans we tend to focus on what we lack versus what we already have. Even in our marriage relationships, we tend to focus on what's not going great instead of what is.

I (Gary) want to encourage you to focus on your strengths as a couple. The strongest marriages that last the longest are often made up of partners who focus on their strengths.

Success is achieved by developing our strengths,
not by eliminating our weaknesses.

—Marilyn vos Savant

What are the strengths in your marriage? Another way to ask this is to consider, "What do we do well as a couple?" Are you great financial planners? Maybe you show each other a lot of physical affection, or you work well as a team. Or perhaps you enjoy taking walks, going hiking, or playing sports together.

Can you teach a fun and lively Bible study together at church? Are you great at leading a small group for your kids and their friends? Do both of you play a musical instrument? Are you great at remodeling an older home—making all the decisions about the fixtures, floor plan, landscaping, and tile together? (This would kill my wife—Norma—and me, but maybe you and your spouse do this well.)

Figure out what you can do together that makes you both feel energized and maximizes your giftedness as a couple—and then do more of it!

Don't Forget the Fun Factor

Think about the last time you really laughed together, had fun together, and enjoyed each other. When was the last time you went on a date or just relaxed together? What were you doing?

Maybe a few years ago you pulled out a card game, and you realized that he loved connecting with you while playing this game. You liked it too, but you haven't pulled out the game since. Time can fly by without the two of you enjoying each other.

I (Gary) can remember the days Norma and I had teenagers in the house. Too many times, doing something energizing and fun as a couple was the exact thing we eliminated from of our lives. It often seemed more important to be at one more soccer game over the weekend than to spend time together as a couple.

Now make sure you hear me: There is nothing wrong with attending your child's soccer game. However, it's important to spend time with each other as a couple, focusing on what you do well together.

If you've been so focused on your differences that you've forgotten what you love to do together, refresh your memories. Explore the interests and activities that add joy to your marriage, and when you find them, hold on to them! Don't eliminate those activities. Enjoy them!

Two Are Better Than One

Criticism can actually bring on more of what you don't like about your husband and his behaviors. But praise and appreciation encourages more of what you do like. Don't overlook what's great about your spouse or your marriage.

I (Gary) know I often become aware of this after the fact. Norma has a very detailed personality and loves routine and order. I'm anything but that. I am a free spirit and love spontaneity and change. One way these opposite tendencies showed themselves was in our restaurant choices. Whenever Norma would eat out for breakfast, she always chose the same place. I, on the other hand, wasn't at the same place twice in three years. Now I would have much rather had Norma join me in trying a different restaurant every day in Branson. But instead, she kept her routine, and I either joined her or she ate breakfast alone.

I realized that I could either try to change Norma's personality or accept and embrace our differences. I preferred to see our marriage as beautifully balanced because of our personalities. Thanks to our differences, we were quite a team running our ministry together. Norma was able to balance the checkbook, stay home, and keep the house running efficiently while I traveled all over the country and ate in a different state many days of the month. This arrangement worked well for us.

I'm guessing that your marriage is made up of a beautiful blend of colors as well with its own unique combination of strengths and growth areas. Embrace both, but always focus on your strengths! Your differences—personality, gender, and otherwise—can bring a beautiful balance in your marriage relationship. As you understand yourself better, and also seek to understand who your husband has been uniquely created to be, you can then learn how to deal with these differences in your marriage relationship. Ultimately, you can then allow each of your beautiful colors to shine.

Focusing on the Positives in Your Marriage

1. Realize that human beings are more inclined to look at the negative aspects than the positive aspects in any situation or relationship. Purposefully work against that tendency in your marriage.
2. Instead of focusing on a small negative aspect, try to see several positive things in your marriage that contribute to the whole picture.
3. When you see something nice or beneficial in your marriage, try to focus on it and bring it to your partner's attention right away. Otherwise, after a few seconds you may just forget about it. Don't miss opportunities to focus and comment on the positive!

Key Four: Connecting Spiritually

◇◇◇◇◇◇◇◇◇◇◇◇◇◇◇◇◇   ♥ ♥ ♥   ◇◇◇◇◇◇◇◇◇◇◇◇◇◇◇◇◇

Relating at the Soul Level

I'll never forget the day my (Erin's) sweet friend Misty revealed to me how her inner longing for a soul mate had impacted her life in a way she could never have imagined. She wasn't exactly out cruising around looking for a soul mate—she was at the grocery store. After years away, she had moved back to her hometown and crossed paths with an old friend while picking up a gallon of milk. Tom was actually someone she had dated during high school. The town was still small enough that they repeatedly ran into one another and ended up meeting for coffee just to catch up. They seemed to reconnect so easily—there was a mutual understanding, a feeling of being "on the same wavelength" with someone, even a sort of mystical emotional connection. It was as if they understood and valued the same things and sensed that almost intuitively. Isn't that what being soul mates means?

Misty thought it did, and unexpectedly finding that connection drew her into their relationship rather quickly. In fact, the soul connection was paired with a physical chemistry that was almost intoxicating. Maybe this is what she had longed for and not found. Everything was fantastic it seemed, except for the fact that Misty and Tom were married—to other partners.

Misty's heart and soul were longing for something, something that wasn't at that moment being fulfilled in her marriage or in her relation-ship with God. What began as a heartfelt connection to another person ended up in an affair that nearly destroyed two families.

When Misty poured out her story to me, I could see how her heart longed for connection. I could also see the painful destruction that a connection outside of marriage had caused. She felt disillusioned and confused—wasn't connecting with a soul mate what marriage was all about? She'd certainly heard that idea a lot—even from two high-profile celebrities who'd left their original marriages to pursue new soul mates.

I can understand Misty's confusion and hurt. Remember what I shared about the early years of our marriage—the disconnect over differences? Well, those negative feelings that developed toward Greg coupled with a longing for something more led me to believe that we couldn't connect at any kind of deep level. (We were having enough problems with surface issues and conflicts!)

Scripture teaches that our soul mate is not our human marriage partner. Total connectedness, total understanding, and total love come from God and God alone!

—Steve Bell, "Soul Connections"

I look back now and see that God was giving me a chance to learn that the connection I was most made for was with Him, and not, ulti-mately with Greg. As I kept growing in my walk with God, I found myself better able to free Greg from my unrealistic expectations and instead form a healthier basis for a deeper connection with him. Don't get me wrong. I still have expectations of Greg (and God does too!). But I'm learning not to let disappointment with these expectations push me to look in a direction other than God.

So what does it mean to have a spiritual connection? Well, the New Testament uses the word *spiritual* (in Greek, *pneumatikos*) twenty-six times.[1] In general, it has to do with the human spirit, the part of you that mirrors God's image and is most made for God.[2] As a Christian, I know that my most important and basic spiritual connection is with God through Jesus Christ. I gain truth and insight from His Word, complain and cry out to Him when life is hard, rejoice and thank Him when life is good, seek to know and follow Him, and am comforted, guided, and taught by the Holy Spirit living inside of me. This life-giving spiritual connection can also be one of the highlights of marriage—to share *together* this kind of connection with God and *together* be His instruments.

Marriages that lack spiritual connection almost always create pain and loneliness—and we'll address that later in the chapter. But for now we're going to look at how we can grow in our own connection with God, how we can encourage and support our husbands in their spiritual lives, and what we can do to foster genuine spiritual connection as a couple. It's a little different than the sometimes mystical idea of having a soul mate.

Strengthening Your Own Connection with Christ

In chapter 2 we talked about the aspect of nourishing our souls—that beginning and continuing a life with Christ is the basis for living life to the full. And we pointed out that abiding—keeping connected with God—impacts everything else in life, including our relationship with our husbands. Another important aspect of our relationship with Jesus that can affect our connection with Him is our identity. If we search for our identity in our relationships with our spouses or children, or anything else for that matter, we diminish our vital connection with Him. We tend to pour our energy into preserving what makes us feel valued and important, hoping for a great result, instead of resting in our identity in Christ. I (Erin) have learned this lesson in different seasons of my life as I've tried desperately to find my identity in other places.

Prior to knowing Jesus, grades and achievements were my identity. Growing up I was always the girl who received the highest grades in the class. I can vividly remember my third-grade teacher, Mrs. Porter, announcing that only one person had received a perfect score on the math test. Without missing a beat, every student in the class began to chant "Erin . . . Erin" in unison. I was embarrassed, and yet this acclaim just drove me harder to succeed.

Throughout my childhood, whenever I needed affirmation and a sense of self-worth, I looked to my academic achievements. I graduated from high school at the top of my class with a 4.3 grade-point average. I also landed a full-tuition scholarship to any college in the state of Arizona. On top of that, I held a thirty-hour-per-week job, played sports, and was involved in almost every club conceivable. On the outside I looked successful, but insecurity and low self-esteem lurked deep inside. So I worked even harder.

During my freshman year in college, I continued striving to succeed. But for the first time in my life, my efforts weren't producing the expected results. I actually failed a chemistry class and lost my college scholarship. This failure devastated me academically, but worse, it touched a deep part of my soul—my very being was shattered. If I had always been the smart one, what did failing academically say about me?

What happened to me happens to many women. We look to relationships, possessions, accomplishments, and appearance as the sources of our identity. But the truth is, these things can never fill the gaping holes in our souls or provide the spiritual connection we're longing for. When they become the center of our lives and identities, they become idols, usurping the place only God should fill.

I was so relieved when I invited Jesus into my life during my sophomore year at GCU and learned that none of these things could ever truly fulfill me. Jesus is the ultimate source of our fulfillment in life. As our Creator and Savior, He is the only one who can affirm our value and meet our deepest needs. When our identities are anchored in Christ, the peace, freedom, and joy He gives us aren't dependent on our husbands or our marriages—or anything else!

Finding our identity and fulfillment in God is the starting point for a deeper spiritual connection with Him. You may be asking, "What does this mean and how do I do it?" Maybe a practical way to start is by thinking about what it is you are longing for. Do you want to be noticed, affirmed, and loved? You're not alone. We women long for thoughtful and loving actions and words directed from another—especially our husbands—toward us, reminding us that we matter and that they want us. Maybe you'll identify with Sandy who struggled with that basic need in her own marriage.

I had been married to Wayne for eleven months, and things weren't going well. I met with a mentor and told her, "I need you to help me with my self-image. But I'm pretty sure I know what the problem is. If Wayne could just do a better job of making me feel loved, I think everything would be all right."

To her everlasting credit, my mentor didn't burst out laughing. Instead, she shared a profound truth with me. "Sandy, if all Wayne did for twenty-four hours a day was sit around and try to make you feel loved, he couldn't do it because that's not his job; it's God's job."

I was dumbfounded. I had been trying to draw from Wayne what only God could supply! My mentor said I needed to renew my mind (Romans 12:1–2) and encouraged me to memorize Psalm 139. Everything went pretty well as I plowed through the psalm, until I came to verse 13: "You created my inmost being; you knit me together in my mother's womb."

I couldn't get past that verse. I said to God, "Wait just a minute! This verse says You *chose* to make me the way I am. You *chose* this nose and this hair. I'm sorry, but what were You thinking? You can't have *chosen* to make me this way! I know Your Word says You don't make mistakes, but I'm here to tell You I'm Your first one!"

I argued and argued with Him, but gradually His Word began to penetrate my mind, and I learned to rest in the fact that He created me. Wayne will tell you that he's married to a totally different person now—because I know I'm not only loved; I was created by a God who chose to make me just the way I am!"

◇◇◇◇◇◇◇◇◇◇◇◇◇◇◇◇◇◇◇◇◇ ♥♥♥ ◇◇◇◇◇◇◇◇◇◇◇◇◇◇◇◇◇◇◇◇◇

I try so hard to please you
To be the love that fills you up
I try to pour on sweet affection
But I think you got a broken cup

—David Wilcox, "Break in the Cup"

◇◇◇◇◇◇◇◇◇◇◇◇◇◇◇◇◇◇◇◇◇ ♥♥♥ ◇◇◇◇◇◇◇◇◇◇◇◇◇◇◇◇◇◇◇◇◇

Ladies, this is the kind of talking-and-hearing, praying-and-meditating, arguing-and-listening kind of relationship we need with God. Only God can fill our need to be loved, accepted, affirmed, and fully known. He is the true lover of our souls, the one with whom we can find the deepest and most true connection. But if you want to know and enjoy God like this, you need to pursue Him. Connection with God, like any relationship, takes a commitment of time and focus. Similar to what we mentioned in chapter 2, here are some practical ways to strengthen your connection with Christ.

- Find or create a niche of time in your daily routine that's just for Him. Talk to Him in prayer; read His Word with a listening, responsive, willing-to-obey heart.
- Continually renew your mind in the truth, as Romans 12:2 says. Remember that you belong to Jesus, and your identity and worth are in Him alone.
- Seek to become the person God created you to be rather than comparing yourself to others. Ask God to mold you into the image of His Son and show you daily what it means to be like Him.
- Ask God continually to fill you with His Spirit so that you can love your husband and others the way He does. Allow the Holy Spirit to grow His fruit in your life.
- Search your heart daily before God. Bring your shortcomings, failures, and sins to Him frequently, asking Him to forgive you and enable you to live in a way that pleases Him.
- Join a Bible study to grow in your faith or seek out a mentoring relationship with a Christ-like woman who can help you strengthen your relationship with Jesus.

When you are pursuing Christ and receiving from Him, you are so much less likely to be overcome by a need to fill the gaping hole of connection with someone who can never keep it permanently filled up. And you are more free to give to your husband, not just demand that you receive. It is this essential spiritual connection with God that enables us to become the wholehearted wives He intendes us to be.

Encouraging Your Husband's Faith

As a young wife, I (Erin) can remember the disappointment I felt in Greg as the spiritual leader of our family. Often he didn't lead the way I thought he should, so I would just take over and do the job I felt was his. The result was major resentment and bitterness on my part and frustration and failure on his.

I often hear other women express the same complaint. Many wives feel angry, resentful, resigned, and confused about what to do with husbands who seem religiously bored, spiritually absent, or unwilling to lead their families toward Christ. One wife described her frustration:

> I had visions of my husband leading Bible studies in our home, taking a leadership role at church, praying with me over our problems, and talking about godly things with our children. Instead, he stumbled over grace at mealtime and hardly ever brought up the subject of God or faith or church.[3]

Why are many husbands passive when it comes to leading their families spiritually? Statistics indicate that it's a growing epidemic in our country:

- On any given Sunday there are about 10 million more adult women than men in America's churches.[4]
- In 2008, about 90 percent of American men said they believe in God or a "higher power," and five out of six call themselves Christians.[5] But only one out of six attends church on a given Sunday.[6] The average man accepts the reality of Jesus Christ, but fails to see any value in going to church.[7]
- An estimated 10 percent of US churches are able to establish or maintain a vibrant men's ministry.[8]

For some, the root of this failure to lead spiritually may be that husbands aren't nurturing a deeper personal relationship with Christ. Perhaps that's also why many husbands seem reluctant to take the lead in keeping their marriages strong, parenting their children, managing household responsibilities, or making financial decisions. When husbands aren't fulfilling their God-ordained roles as the spiritual leaders of the home, they may fail to step up in other areas of the marriage as well.

If this is the situation in your marriage (and this may not be true for your marriage), what can you do? The answer isn't to complain more or criticize your husband. Nor is it to resign yourself to his passivity. Instead, the answer lies in allowing God to work on your husband and controlling what you can: *yourself.*

There are several powerful steps you can take to encourage your husband's spiritual life and leadership:

1. Guard your heart by expressing gratitude. King Solomon, the author of the wisdom books in the Bible, wrote, "Above all else, guard your heart, for it is the wellspring of life" (Proverbs 4:23). To encourage your husband's faith, you must first shore up your own heart. One aspect of guarding your heart means that you keep it from closing or from shutting down. Anger, resentment, and apathy are signs of a closed heart. The best weapon against these painful emotions is gratitude. At first this may seem trivial. But trust us, gratitude is a powerful defense against a closed heart. Try noticing what you appreciate about your husband. We love how one author put it: "Maybe your husband is not delivering three-point sermons every night, but he faithfully provides, serves, helps, and loves. Have you grown blind to his benevolent heart?"[9]

Look for things your husband is doing right. Then write them down in a gratitude journal and share them with your husband—daily, if possible. Hebrews 3:13 tells us to "encourage one another daily, as long as it is called Today, so that none of you may be hardened by sin's deceitfulness." You're guarding your heart when you actively notice and express gratitude for your blessings and the many gifts God has given you.

Pastor John Piper suggests that our attitude needs to be,

> Okay, this may never change in my husband. I hope it does,
> but it may never change; and I'm not going to lock in on this
> shortcoming as the only thing I think about with him. Instead,
> I will try to love him, bless him, enjoy him for the things about
> him that I delight in, and all the while be praying and model-
> ing what I hope he will become for me.[10]

A great way to bolster your gratitude is to take the Thirty-Day
Husband Encouragement Challenge found at *www.reviveourhearts
.com.*[11]

2. Are you following? One of our favorite Scripture verses says,

> How can you say to your brother, "Let me take the speck out
> of your eye," when all the time there is a plank in your own
> eye? You hypocrite, first take the plank out of your own eye,
> and then you will see clearly to remove the speck from your
> brother's eye. (Matthew 7:4–5)

To encourage your husband as a spiritual leader, you first need to
focus on your role as a follower or helper. Start by asking yourself this
difficult question: "Do I let my husband lead?" This could be the log
in your eye.

This isn't about assigning blame. Your husband truly might be passive or withdrawn. His lack of leadership may result from the absence
of a strong male role model growing up. Or he may find it difficult to
lead because of an emotional wound from childhood, an introverted
personality, or some other issue. You might be a strong woman with
a take-charge personality that he finds a bit intimidating. Or perhaps
you unintentionally mother him, treat him like a child, make him feel

incompetent, constantly question or undermine his decisions, step in or take over with the kids, answer questions for him, or make decisions without consulting him. Whatever the case may be, a man is often reluctant to lead because he has a wife who is reluctant to follow.

I (Erin) struggle with this! I'm a strong, independent woman. Although this comes in handy when Greg is traveling and I need to take over at home, it doesn't work so well when he returns. Then I wonder why he isn't leading. I now realize that I'm probably not leaving him much of a choice. Following his lead is not always easy because often I'm not aware when I have stepped in and taken over. Really reflect on this and think about what it would look like for you to support his attempts, even if you think you have a better way to do it.

Pray about this issue and search your heart for insight about your role as a follower. Then give your husband space to lead.

3. Respect your husband. Ephesians 5:33 specifically calls wives to respect their husbands. We believe the key element needed to respect your man is one of the most dreaded, misunderstood, and hotly debated concepts in the Bible and in our Christian culture: *submission.*

Now don't roll your eyes or throw down the book in disgust. If you're like me (Erin), I've been both offended and alarmed at how this word is often wrongly defined and misapplied within marriage. Ever since the apostle Paul wrote about wives submitting to their husbands, countless men have used this instruction to control or dominate their wives. Some believe that submission is simply about blind obedience. Others suggest it's about wives denying their opinions, desires, needs, and feelings. As Allison Stevens explains,

> This false concept of submission is often used to manipulate and control women. It advocates quiet obedience and subservience, and denies a woman's irreplaceable value in her marital relationship. It also ignores the potential for a man

to be heavy-handed and unloving in his attempt to be the "ruler" of his home.[12]

Sadly, many women have been encouraged to submit to an abusive husband. I used to cringe at the word *submit* because I wondered if I was being asked to be a weak doormat, complying timidly with my husband's every wish. But that isn't the case. So let's have an honest discussion about what submission really means and how we can use it to honor and respect each other and our marriage.

What specifically does submission mean for a husband and wife? Ephesians 5:21–33 gives us the best answer. In verse 21, Paul stated that we should "submit [ourselves] to one another out of reverence for Christ." In essence, the true foundation of submission in marriage is a husband and wife submitting to the roles God has given them out of reverence, or respect, for Christ. It becomes essential, then, to understand what those roles and actions involve.

Let's start with the role God gave to men. To husbands Paul issued this charge:

> Husbands, love your wives, just as Christ loved the church
> and gave himself up for her to make her holy, cleansing her
> by the washing with water through the word, and to present
> her to himself as a radiant church, without stain or wrinkle or
> any other blemish, but holy and blameless. In this same way,
> husbands ought to love their wives as their own bodies. He
> who loves his wife loves himself. After all, no one ever hated
> his own body, but he feeds and cares for it, just as Christ does
> the church—for we are members of his body. "For this reason a
> man will leave his father and mother and be united to his wife,
> and the two will become one flesh." This is a profound mys-
> tery—but I am talking about Christ and the church. However,

each one of you also must love his wife as he loves himself.
(verses 25–33)

Paul's teaching to husbands here was revolutionary. He wasn't a male chauvinist. He didn't devalue women. He wasn't trying to encourage men to dominate women. Consider the Greco-Roman culture two thousand years ago. Most men viewed women as nothing more than possessions—something they owned. Instead, Paul's message was radical in that he elevated wives to a place where they are to be loved as Christ loves the church. And Jesus died for the church!

Dan Lacich's encouragement to men explains this point so well:

Husbands are to submit their desires to their [wives] by serving [them] to the point of death. Husbands are to "die to themselves" and do all they can to help their wives become the beautiful, precious bride that Christ also has in mind for the church. For most men the idea of laying down their life for their wife will immediately go to fighting off an attacker or pushing her away from an oncoming bus while you take a grill to the chest. The chances of either of those opportunities happening are astronomically slim. What is far more likely is that husbands will be asked to die to themselves and submit to their wives by doing dishes, caring for the kids so she can have a day away, ironing her clothes, or making her lunch. It includes helping her achieve her dreams and become all that God made her to be. It means putting her first.[13]

Just as Christ gave His life for His bride (the church) in loving self-sacrifice, husbands are called to lay down their lives for their wives. A husband's love should be sacrificial, cherishing, and nourishing. A man should love his wife in the same way he loves his own body.

To wives Paul wrote,

Wives, submit yourselves to your husbands as to the Lord. For
the husband is the head of the wife as Christ is the head of the
church, his body, of which he is the Savior. Now as the church
submits to Christ, so also wives should submit to their husbands in everything. . . . And the wife must respect her husband. (Ephesians 5:22–24, 33)

First, Paul never said it's the husband's responsibility to make his
wife submit. The Greek word for "submission" is *hupotasso*, which means
"to subject one's self."[14] *Submission is voluntary*—God is telling wives to
voluntarily follow their husbands' lead. Author Mary Kassian agrees:

A husband does not have the right to demand or extract
submission from his wife. Submission is *her* choice—her
responsibility. It is *not* his right! Not ever. She is to "submit
herself"—deciding when and how to submit is her call.[15]

Submission is a choice. A wife submits to her husband out of her
own free will in response to her love and commitment to the Lord. She
accepts her husband's role as the leader of their family out of respect
for God's command: "You wives must accept the authority of your
husbands" (1 Peter 3:1, NLT). Submission is less about an action or a
set of behaviors as it is about a *mind-set*—it's an attitude of the heart.
We really like the way Mary Kassian describes this conviction:

Submission boils down to having a spirit of amenability. It means
being soft, receptive, responsive, and agreeable. Because of the
misconceptions surrounding the definition of *submission*, I actually prefer to use the term *amenability*. *Amenability* comes from
the French *amener* (to lead). An amenable woman is "leadable" as
opposed to "ungovernable." She's responsive to input and likely

to cooperate. . . . So "what it looks like" on an on-going basis, is that I am soft, receptive, and agreeable toward my husband. I love responding to his lead. I respect who God created him to be as a man—and support his efforts to provide godly oversight for our family. I respect the position of responsibility that goes along with being a husband and father. *Respect* is probably the best word to describe what submission looks like in my marriage.[16]

Mutual submission boils down to love and respect. A husband is to love his bride as Christ loves the church—he is to die to himself and love her wholeheartedly. A wife is to respect her husband and voluntarily place herself under her husband's God-given leadership role. She is to follow his lead and serve him wholeheartedly out of love.

What If My Husband Is Not a Believer?
Gary Smalley

You might be reading this book and thinking, *All of this information is good, but you don't understand my circumstances. I'm married to an unbeliever.*

One of the questions I often hear from women in unequally yoked marriages is, "Do I still have to submit to my husband if he is an unbeliever?" (The apostle Paul addressed being "yoked together with unbelievers" in 2 Corinthians 6:14–18.) First Peter 3 tells women,

> Be submissive to your husbands so that, if any of them do not believe . . ., they may be won over without words . . . when they see the purity and reverence of your lives. Your beauty should . . . be that of your inner

self, the unfading beauty of a quiet and gentle spirit, which is of great worth in God's sight. (verses 1–3, 4)

The more an unbelieving husband sees his wife respond with the love and power Christ gives, the more attractive her lifestyle will be to him. When he experiences her interacting with him with the love of Jesus, he will brush up against Jesus. When an unbelieving man experiences his wife extending forgiveness, seeking to meet his needs, blessing him, and praying for him, there is no greater chance of influencing him. However, remember that the only person you can control is you. The Holy Spirit is the only one who can move and impact hearts. Give Him room to do His job while you serve as a continuous conduit of love to your spouse.

I recently listened to a radio broadcast with three women who have been in your situation. In the interview, Lynn, Dineen, and Darla discussed many of the difficulties of being married to nonbelievers, and the women reflected on the loneliness they sometimes feel. Dineen emphasized how vital it was for her to find others on that same journey:

> [Finding a group] for the spiritually mismatched . . . was the beginning of realizing that I could do this— that I could walk through my marriage in a way that would honor God and would help my husband—that I could be a helper to him still, and not hinder him, and still grow in my faith.

We pray you'll find this type of community even as you're reading this book. If you're reading it as part of a group, others around you may be in the same circumstance.

4. Model a vibrant faith. As you seek to encourage your husband's faith, your battle cry should be 1 Corinthians 16:13–14: "Be on your guard; stand firm in the faith; be [women] of courage; be strong. Do everything in love." First and foremost, stand firm in the faith. In other words, it's your job to grow more like Christ. Some women have given away this responsibility to their husbands. Your faith is your responsibility.

For me (Erin), attending Bible study has been a joy. I often feel sorry for Greg because he doesn't have the luxury of attending a group during the day. But I do. So I often will share what I'm learning. I do encourage him to attend the men's group at our church, even though this means a little morning inconvenience for me having to drive kids to school. However, in the big picture, is this really a true inconvenience? Ladies, we must go out of our way, sometimes with a small sacrifice, to help our men get to groups (accountability, prayer, Bible study or other men's group) so they can reap the benefits we do from studying with our sisters in Christ. For my introvert, encouragement is necessary—not manipulation, but straight encouragement and often prayer.[18]

5. Pray for your husband. We know this advice sounds cliché, but prayer is powerful. Stormie Omartian explains the power of praying for your husband this way:

> Something amazing happens to our hearts when we pray for another person. The hardness melts. We become able to get beyond the hurts, and forgive. We even end up loving the person we are praying for. It's miraculous! It happens because when we pray we enter into the presence of God and He fills us with His Spirit of love. . . . I've seen women with no feelings of love for their husbands find that as they prayed, over time, those

feelings came. Sometimes they felt differently even after the first heartfelt prayer. [19]

Please don't think that all men are struggling spiritually. Many men have a vibrant walk with the Lord. However, all men can use some encouragement and support while balancing work, family, and us (their wholehearted wives) in order to continue pursuing God. If you do have a husband who is struggling in this area, ask the Lord to help you meet him with compassion. Pray fervently for him, but release him to the Lord. The Lord can change his heart. And remember, men are really good at sniffing out attempts to manipulate. Try to put yourself in their shoes—some men work all day or all night—and frankly it may not seem super appealing to sit with a group of men to pray or to come home and open their Bible (I'm not making excuses—just trying to point out the reality.) Be creative in your encouragement, focus on modeling a vibrant faith, and as God shows up—you never know the impact it will all have on your husband's personal walk with the Lord.

Nurturing a Thriving Spiritual Connection in Your Marriage

Now that you've learned how to strengthen your relationship with Christ and encourage your husband's faith, let's look at how you can build a strong shared spiritual relationship in your marriage.

We really like David Schnarch's definition of *intimacy*: "the process of open . . . disclosure of core aspects of [ourselves] in the presence of a partner."[20] This open disclosure reflects the process of opening our hearts to one another. Spiritual intimacy, or connection, takes place when a husband and wife open their hearts to the Lord as well as each other. Unfortunately, many couples feel close to their spouses in every way except spiritually. In this area they often feel disconnected or alone.

Usually this spiritual disconnect creeps into the other areas of their relationship and impacts their overall level of intimacy and connection.

The way we mutually experience closeness with God and with our husbands is through our relationship with Jesus Christ. This three-way spiritual connection creates a powerful emotional closeness with each other. As we grow closer to the Lord and each other, we strengthen this spiritual connection.

Marriage expert Dr. Gary J. Oliver, Executive Director of The Center for Relationship Enrichment at John Brown University, highlights some of the differences between a Christ-centered marriage and a marriage that is simply between two Christians.[21] Remember that you can encourage what can be done jointly but control only your own spiritual growth and responses.

Marriage Between Two Christians	Christ-Centered Marriage
Jesus is valued. (A fan)	Jesus is Lord. (A follower)
Problem-focused	Growth-focused
You are here for me. (Self-focused)	I am here for you. (Other-focused)
I pray alone.	We pray together.
Reads the Bible. (Hearer)	Applies the Bible. (Doer)
Conditional love (Contract marriage)	Unconditional love (Covenant marriage)
I focus on me and you.	I focus on us.
I want you to make *me* happy.	I choose to make *you* happy.
I hear you.	I listen to you.
I want to be understood.	I choose to understand.
I want to be served.	I seek opportunities to serve.
I assume the worst.	I assume the best.
I pray periodically.	I pray without ceasing.
Individual spirituality	Shared spirituality
Lord, change my spouse.	Lord, change me.
Happy	Joyful
I "should" sacrifice.	I enjoy sacrifice.
Has passion	Passionate
Decisional forgiveness	Emotional forgiveness

If you want a more loving relationship with your husband, focus on developing these Christ-centered qualities in your marriage. But you can't reach this goal by working harder to change your husband. The key is becoming more Christ-like yourself.

Some basics Norma and I (Gary) have learned over the years about nurturing our spiritual relationship are pretty simple yet profound. Here are some practical steps that have helped us:

Read the Bible together. Even if you just read a verse a day, the Word of God has power beyond anything else you can read as a couple.

Talk about spiritual things. Share what you both got out of the Sunday-morning sermon. Talk about what God is teaching you. Admit your own struggles. And confess your sins to each other (James 5:16).

Attend church together. It's easy (especially after the kids are gone) to get out of the routine of attending church every week. Hebrews 10:25 says, "Let us not give up meeting together, as some are in the habit of doing, but let us encourage one another—and all the more as you see the Day approaching." We were made to be in community with believers! So find a church that you both love and try to attend every week.

Join a marriage small group. Our (Gary and Norma's) small group might be a little different from the typical small group. In our small group, we're all empty-nesters. We talk about our family dynamics, our children, and our grandchildren. We share our health concerns, our career decisions, and our marriage issues. Sometimes we refer to these couples as our 9-1-1 group because we call a group meeting if there's an emergency in our marriages or families. It has been more than help-ful—even life giving—to be able to turn to one another for support in our times of need. Look for a group of believers who will encourage you and your husband to grow in your faith and your relationship as a couple. Greg and I (Erin) have always been in a weekly small group that supports each couple's marriage. Since moving to Colorado, this has been more difficult for us but we still are part of a fabulous marriage group that meets monthly. When we get to meet with these wonderful couples, it feels like oxygen to our souls. Being part of a community of believers is key to growing together as well as individually.

Serve together. As a marriage team, look for ways to serve together. We love Mark Batterson's encouragement in *Wild Goose Chase*: "If you're in a spiritual slump, let me give you a prescription: go on a [missions] trip."[22] You could go on a missions trip to help rebuild a devastated area or care for orphans. Every community has many opportunities to serve: soup kitchens, food pantries, care homes, work projects, you name it. Pray together about where God might want you to be His hands and feet. We (Greg and Erin) truly believe that there is greater purpose in a Christian marriage—He brought you together and now you share the mutual purpose of glorifying God through your lives. Together you can use your individual characteristics and your unique combination of experiences, calling, and spiritual gifting to contribute to God's kingdom. As Greg and I teach marriage seminars together or sit with a couple experiencing a crisis, we know we have found a shared purpose. There is not a time we feel more satisfied in our marriage relationship. I encourage you to continue searching for ways you can work together to accomplish God's purposes in this world.

Memorize Scripture together. I (Gary) love to write God's Word on my heart. Nothing has been better for our marriage than memorizing Scripture together. Especially as of late, Norma will come up with a verse pertaining to whatever we might be dealing with in our current circumstances. We memorize it and even check with each other to make sure that we're putting it into practice.

I (Erin) love when I hear my father-in-law share what he and Norma have been memorizing. He beams with pride as he talks about how he is watching God's Word changing Norma. (Now I'm not sure why he doesn't share how it's changing him—but I do know that he is proud of her.)

Pray over each other. You can't get any more intimate than praying together as a couple. I'm sure you've heard the phrase "People who pray together stay together." According to a national survey, the happiest married couples pray together.[23] There's nothing more heart-warming than falling asleep listening to your husband's prayers for you or hearing your husband call out to God on your behalf in a time of need. Erin will often call me (Greg) on the road and ask if she can pray for me. It warms my heart and makes me feel loved.

Study together. Do a Bible study or read a devotional book together, or work through a study independently and then discuss it together. There are hundreds of workbooks and devotionals—some designed especially for married couples—that can greatly add to your intentional time together and deepen your spiritual connection.

Count your blessings. Set aside time frequently to thank God for what He has given you—especially your husband.

Remember that these are only suggestions to guide you as a couple in building a shared spiritual relationship. They aren't intended as items to check off your to-do list or to make you feel guilty if you don't do them regularly. We can't guarantee you'll experience a deeper spiritual intimacy as a result of following these steps. But spending intentional time as a couple to focus on your relationship with Christ and develop a hunger for Him together can help to deepen your spiritual connection as a couple. If what you want is more loving relationship with your husband, this is an essential place to start.

I (Erin) can truly say that this chapter on spiritual connection in your marriage is one of the most important concepts in the book. It's foundational for a marriage that thrives. More than likely, as you read through this chapter, you thought, *I'd really love to talk with my husband about strengthening our spiritual connection.* The great news is that in the next chapter, you'll discover communication skills and methods that can help you initiate that conversation.

✕✕✕✕✕✕✕✕✕✕✕✕✕ ♥ ♥ ♥ ✕✕✕✕✕✕✕✕✕✕✕✕✕

A Matter of the Heart

Over the past thirty years of speaking about marriage, I (Gary) have asked couples to name one thing they believe could improve their marriages above everything else. Without exception, the answer from more than three hundred thousand people has been "communication."[1] This perception is apparently shared by the younger generation as well.

One day I happened to be in a classroom of fifth-grade girls. So I decided to conduct an informal survey. "Picture yourself married," I said. "You're a year into it, and things aren't going well. What do you need to improve?" Even in fifth grade, the most common female response was "communication."

Why is communication in marriage so difficult? It can seem like a major struggle just to have a meaningful conversation with the very person who is supposed to be our closest confidant. Why do husbands and wives seem to have so much trouble expressing their deepest thoughts and feelings to each other? Some of these reasons may have to do with personality or gender differences that we've touched on in previous chapters. In this chapter we'll look at one other major factor that influences communication styles and then share some strategic ideas that have been used, evaluated, and refined over decades of working with couples on this pivotal aspect of marriage.

Healthy communication not only fosters deeper understanding between you and your spouse, but it's essential to a more loving relationship. By learning to communicate better yourself, you can foster better communication in your marriage.

Communication Patterns in Our Families of Origin

Before we get into communication strategies, it is very helpful to realize that we've all been influenced in myriad ways by our families of origin. What we experienced within the four walls of the homes we grew up in often determines our communication patterns as adults.

What was communication like in your family? Did you tend to yell at one another or withdraw during conflicts? Did one of your parents dominate the other verbally? Did your family fight fair, or were putdowns and old baggage a frequent part of conversations or disagreements? Did one parent stuff and deny, only to explode later? Was it safe to verbalize feelings and needs, or were they minimized or mocked?

Greg and I (Erin) grew up in families that could not have been more opposite when it came to communication. My family would often yell about an issue, get it all out, and then it was over. Greg's family tended to be on the quieter end of the spectrum when it came to communicating. They would often hold family meetings where they strategically talked through issues or sometimes, in order to keep harmony, they would not address issues at all.

Within the first months of our marriage, I really couldn't understand why Greg wouldn't engage with me around issues. I actually would subconsciously pick fights in order to connect. I believed that was how connection happened. I had a lot to learn over those first few years, and although I am definitely not perfect in my communication attempts, I've come a long way. Greg has too. He really became aware of his tendency to avoid issues because he would be afraid my reaction would be negative. Our communication tends to be much healthier now than it was the first few years of our marriage.

You may have never thought through ramifications of being raised with differing communication styles. It's helpful to reflect and gain understanding in order to make needed adjustments. Of course, we begin with ourselves, as wholehearted wives, and look at how we influence the communication patterns in our marriage.

The communication patterns you grew up with don't have to control you, but you do need to recognize their impact on you and your marriage. Learn to discern between the healthy and unhealthy patterns you experienced growing up, and commit to developing healthy communication patterns in your own marriage.

In the following sections, we'll explore some tried and tested communication tools that have helped hundreds of thousands of couples. First, we'll explore how we communicate with ourselves and process things internally. Then we will take a look at communication from a husband's perspective. We'll finish off by showing you how to get beyond the surface to deeper levels of communication in your marriage, which will ultimately foster greater understanding and intimacy.

The Ins and Outs of Self-talk

Catholic priest and Loyola University theology professor John Powell wrote a landmark book in 1969 titled *Why Am I Afraid to Tell You Who I Am?* He stated at the beginning of the book that at its root, communication means "a process by which someone or something is made common, that is, it is shared."[2] This might include sharing information or sharing a secret, but its real essence, according to Powell, is sharing who you are as a person. That's why communication is fundamental to intimacy in marriage—it is two people sharing their real selves.

But before you can share who you truly are with your husband, you must first know who you are, or as Powell would say, who you are becoming.[3] We're all works in process, not finished products. Communication is about understanding ourselves the best we can, learning to process our thoughts and feelings in healthy ways, and sharing openly with our spouses in a context of trust.

◇◇◇◇◇◇◇◇◇◇◇◇◇◇◇◇◇◇ ♥♥♥ ◇◇◇◇◇◇◇◇◇◇◇◇◇◇◇◇◇◇

If I am anything as a person, it is what I think, judge, feel, value, honour, esteem, love, hate, fear, desire, hope for, believe in, and am committed to. These are the things that define my person, and they are constantly in process, in the process of change.

—John Powell, *Why Am I Afraid to Tell You Who I Am?*

◇◇◇◇◇◇◇◇◇◇◇◇◇◇◇◇◇◇ ♥♥♥ ◇◇◇◇◇◇◇◇◇◇◇◇◇◇◇◇◇◇

Telling Yourself the Truth

Three vital aspects of good communication are identifying, understanding, and dealing with our own emotions. If you need help recognizing your emotions, understanding the needs they reveal, and examining them in light of God's truth, review the ideas we discussed in chapter 2.

Another important aspect of communication involves what we tell ourselves. Psychologists call this *self-talk*. Mental-health professionals say we do this all the time—either positively or negatively—as if replays are continually playing in our minds. I (Erin) was really unaware of many of the conversations I was having within my own mind. I can remember the dark, early morning I was heading out of town to take my counseling licensure examination. As I turned onto the main road, I became aware of the internal conversation that was going on. Although I was driving on my own, I soon realized that I wasn't by myself after all. The conversation was very negative, and it went something like this, "Why am I even bothering to go take this exam? I am not going to pass anyway. I've waited five years since I finished my degree—what an idiot—who does this?" I felt myself panicking a little bit because suddenly I was going to fail this exam that I had spent hours preparing for. What in the world? Where was this message coming from?

As Christians, our goal isn't positive self-talk; it's *truthful* self-talk. Romans 12:2 (NASB) says, "Be transformed by the renewing of your mind, so that you may prove what the will of God is, that which is good and acceptable and perfect." Truthful self-talk means continually filling and renewing our minds with God's truth about ourselves, our husbands, and our circumstances.

Remember that God loves you and that He is committed to forming you into the image of His Son (Romans 8:29). The one whose hallmark is deception, destruction, and accusation is our archenemy Satan (John 8:44; 10:10; Revelation 12:10). So if you tell yourself you're an idiot or a loser or a hopeless cause, that message isn't coming from your heavenly Father. Much like that dark morning in the car when I assumed I was all alone, I quickly realized that the enemy was lurking. As I drove closer to my exam location, a Casting Crowns song came on the radio. The lyrics reminded me to "listen and believe the voice of truth."

Suddenly, it all made sense. I realized the road the enemy was leading me down. It was one of lies, deception, helplessness, and hopelessness. I began claiming the truth and demanding that the enemy leave me alone in Jesus' name!

Peace began to take over my once-panicked heart. The good news was that I passed my exam that day, but the better and more important lesson I learned was to silence the enemy. The devil knows a lot about how the human heart works and the places where we may be vulnerable to his paralyzing lies. Ladies, we must be women of courage and battle the lies of the enemy! Sometimes, with the help of the Lord, we can take him out in one swipe and other times we need to enlist our other wholehearted sisters in Christ to battle with us in prayer to help us speak truth to ourselves.

It is crucial to become aware of the internal dialogue we have going because it has an impact on how we show up in conversations with others—especially with our husbands. Next, we will take a look at how to best succeed in connecting with our spouses through communication.

Encouraging Your Husband to Communicate

A story has been told about the captain of a fishing ship who was getting ready to go on another ten-month deployment.

"Won't you send me just one letter this time?" pleaded his long-suffering wife. "It would mean so much to me to hear from you. I get so worried and lonely when you're gone."

She nagged and nagged until he finally agreed. After he sailed away, his wife waited for news from him. Two months went by. Three months. Eight months. And finally the mail steamer arrived with a letter from her beloved captain. The wife tore it open with trembling fingers and read the following:

Dear wife,
I am here, and you are there.
Sincerely,
Your husband

Like the captain's wife, many women struggle with how to get their husbands to communicate with them—or to at least share more than seven words at a time! We (Gary, Greg, and Erin) often hear wives complain, "He has so much to say to his coworkers or friends, but he doesn't seem interested in talking to me. Why does he tune me out or refuse to talk?"

Have you heard of the legendary horse whisperer, Nicholas Evans?

What about the baby whisperer, Tracy Hogg? Well, I (Greg) am going to make you a "husband whisperer" by helping you decode the mystery of male communication. (Sometimes Erin will add her two cents!) Here are some tips to help you become an expert in encouraging your man to talk to you:

1. Evaluate your communication expectations. Remember, women communicate to connect relationally. Men talk to achieve something—to fix a problem or give advice, for example. Keep this in mind when you talk with your husband. Author Connie Grigsby says, "A woman's expectations often create some of the conflict because her female friends, her sisters, and her coworkers that are female, they get her style of communication and give it back to her."[4] You can defuse conflict and enhance communication in your marriage by accepting the fact that you and your husband have different communication styles.

Author Richard Drobnick explains how a man communicates:

> He is conditioned to listen actively. When a woman initiates conversation he assumes she is seeking his advice or assistance. He engages with the woman, filtering everything she's saying through the lens of, "What can we actually do about this?" Learning to listen patiently—not just passively—doesn't come easily to him.[5]

So don't expect your husband to communicate like your girl-friends, and don't get hurt when he doesn't. Realize that your husband may not know what you're expecting from him. As men, we don't "get" this naturally! Be willing to adjust your expectations accordingly and welcome his input. Remember that being a troubleshooter is the way God designed him.

2. Study your husband's communication patterns. Become an expert in how your husband likes to communicate. When is he most attentive?

At which time of day does he most like to talk? Gather clues by watching how he talks to his friends. What does he talk about? What are his interests? What does he seem to get from those conversations? By studying your husband's conversation behaviors, you might discover some new insights or additional interests you can talk about with him.

3. *Spice up your talks with some conversational foreplay.* You've probably heard the comment that when it comes to sex, women are like Crock-Pots and men are like microwaves. In other words, women warm up slowly, and men are ready in an instant. Well, the reverse is true when it comes to communicating at deep levels. Women can share their feelings fairly quickly, while men take longer to open up and get to a deeper level. So don't call your husband on the phone and jump right into a deep conversation. Instead, ask him a few warm-up questions, such as "How's your day going?" or "What did you do for lunch?"

4. *Pick the right moment and the right activity.* If your husband rejects an invitation to talk, it may be that you chose the wrong time. For instance, most men won't chat about their day right when they come home from work, when the kids are running around, or while they're watching a sporting event on television. You may be excited to tell your husband all about something that happened earlier that day, but first get some food in his belly and let him have some time to relax and unwind. Then do something active if you want him to talk. You may like to sit around and talk while you're sipping on a grande, nonfat peppermint mocha. But remember, men are activity oriented. Try taking a walk while you talk, or take a long drive to get your spouse to open up. At our home this time is called "windshield time." We (Greg and Erin) have found it helpful to even have a set list of questions—Greg loves it when I ask him four particular questions. It definitely helps him get "into the mood" if we are walking or doing an activity together.

The four questions are: How are things going at work? How are things going with your guy friends? How are things going between you and the kids? What is God teaching you as of late?

5. *Don't multitask while talking with your husband.* I know that you can simultaneously have a conversation, answer your child's question, check your text messages, make dinner, and give yourself a pedicure, but your husband can't. It's annoying for men when they try to have a conversation while their wives are doing ten other things. Physician and author Marianne Legato agrees:

> Men don't multitask as well as women do. This may be related to the fact that, in general, women activate more areas in their brain than men do when performing identical tasks. So initiating a discussion while he's watching television or surfing the Internet means you won't get his full attention.[6]

If you want to improve communication with your husband, give him your undivided attention. When he's speaking to you, consciously lay aside other tasks, look into his eyes, and listen to what he's saying. Also stick to one subject at a time. Women seem to easily shift from topic to topic during a conversation. I'm sure this ability originates in the same part of the brain that allows you to multitask so effectively. However, covering multiple topics overwhelms the average man. Deal with one issue or question at a time and then check to see if your husband is ready to move on to a different topic. I (Erin) am guilty of both multitasking and flooding Greg with different topics when we are having a conversation. First and foremost, I have been working on setting the cell phone down—largely because Greg will simply stop talking if I am texting, emailing, looking for recipes, or checking the kids' grades! I hate it when I'm at lunch with a girlfriend and she is constantly checking her cell phone, so why would I not think the impact would be similar with Greg? We've also had numerous conversations about sticking to one topic at a time. Naturally, ladies, we can move quickly from one topic to the next. Literally, one conversation we were having started with the kids not helping around the house enough, to a vacation we needed to plan, and Murphy's soccer tryouts. I knew I'd lost Greg when I saw the emptiness in his eyes. It's helpful to know your audience and just keep in mind that, typically, your husband will not be able to move that quickly through topics. I really try to finish one thought and topic before I move on to the next.

6. *Offer your husband a "diet story."* At one time or another, your husband may wonder, *Why does my wife need to share so many details?* Understand that most men don't realize that women use conversation to explore and organize their thoughts. Men don't really understand that when you tell a story with details, you're discovering how you feel. Sharing details and the finer points of an experience may help you feel connected to your husband, but you're not speaking his language. Right or wrong, this is why he checks out or interrupts you once he has heard enough or feels overwhelmed by a high word count. Offering a "diet story" means that you edit the details or trim back excessive words to keep him engaged in your story.

7. *Soften your approach.* Men are highly sensitive to criticism, disrespect, or failure. If you start the conversation with something like "You . . ." or "We need to talk!" it emotionally shuts us down. According to statistics, the first three minutes of a discussion are a very reliable indicator of how things will go.[7] The key is how you initiate the conversation. If your husband feels that your start-up is harsh, he'll most likely stay silent, exit the conversation, or get angry. A softened start-up is the goal. This means using a gentle voice, kind facial expressions, relaxed body language, and a softer word choice.

King Solomon wrote, "A gentle answer turns away wrath, but a harsh word stirs up anger" (Proverbs 15:1). This is as true in marriage as it is in other relationships. Instead of starting off with an accusing tone, try saying, "There's an issue in our relationship that I believe we can fix together. I'd like to talk about the best way to resolve it."

8. *Accept "fine" as a reasonable answer.* The word *fine* doesn't always have to mean "feelings inside not expressed." I (Erin) never knew I hated this word until I was married. I can remember the first time, as a newly married couple, I walked out of our bedroom with a new outfit on. I asked Greg how he thought I looked. His response was "fine" and immediately I turned around and went and changed my clothes. He couldn't understand why I responded in this manner, but I proceeded to explain how "fine" left me feeling. In many ways, it felt like my outfit was average or tolerable, so when I came across the above definition, it really resonated with me. I have come to learn that there isn't always more going on when "fine" is the response. I've laughed as we have spoken to married couples all over the world, and there has not been a place (including China, Australia, and New Zealand) that the women disagree with me over their distaste of this word. However, when we take into consideration the differences of how we communicate as men and women, it makes sense why this word doesn't typically bother men. Because men tend to communicate more factually and less emotionally, it doesn't mean that they don't care about something if their feelings aren't as deep or multifaceted as yours. They're just wired differently. If you ask them how they feel, "happy" or "sad" may be as descriptive as they can get at the moment.

9. *Resist the urge to correct your husband.* Some women can't allow their husbands to tell a story without stopping them thirteen times to correct inconsequential details:

"It wasn't Tuesday evening; it was Tuesday afternoon."

"It was teal, not green."

"He didn't ride the bus; he took the subway."

I (Greg) like King Solomon's advice: "Even a fool is thought wise if he keeps silent, and discerning if he holds his tongue" (Proverbs 17:28). If you bite your tongue whenever you're tempted to correct your husband in conversation, you'll not only be exercising restraint, but you'll also be considered wise. Solomon said so! Well, I (Erin) might need to continue working on my tongue-biting technique! It is very difficult for me when I know—I mean there is no doubt in my mind—that I asked Greg to do something, that we had a conversation, or that he didn't tell me about a late meeting, to keep my mouth silenced. However, when I started realizing that most of those conversations are a complete waste of time—really "who is right and who is wrong" or "what really happened" isn't going to go anywhere relationally productive—I've gotten much better at holding my tongue. By now, I'm hoping that it's clear to you that we see the world differently, remember things differently, and interpret things differently than our husbands do. To tag on to King Solomon's advice, I'd add, "A wholehearted wife knows when to remain silent and when to speak. She also recognizes which battles are a complete waste of time."

10. Ask for what you want. Many women say they want conversation, but what they really want is someone to listen to and understand them. I (Greg) get that you may not be looking for a solution when you're sharing a problem with your husband. However, men seem genetically programmed to want to solve a problem when presented with one. So instead of making us guess, tell us what you want from the beginning. For instance, you might say, "I don't need a solution. I just want you to listen."

Keep in mind that hinting doesn't usually work. Women are often indirect when communicating with their husbands. Other women can usually pick up subtle messages, but not men.

Take This Hint . . . It's a Gender Issue
Connie Grigsby

The coauthor of *How to Get Your Husband to Listen to You* and *How to Get Your Husband to Talk to You* offers this advice:

> If a woman is speaking to another woman, she can throw out a hint and say something like, "Oh, I am so tired right now. I don't know what we're going to have for dinner." And her girlfriend will say, "Why don't you go out?" or "I'll bring you dinner."
>
> She will get that fishing line that's been thrown out. The girlfriend or sister will take it, understand it, run with it, and give her some feedback, exactly what she wanted to hear. . . .
>
> If a woman says to her husband, "I am so exhausted, I'm not sure what we'll have tonight for dinner because I'm just so tired," he may suggest lasagna because he's not decoding and processing what she is really saying.[8]

It's a lot more effective to just state the actual fact that you're too tired to cook and would like to go out for dinner than to give your husband a veiled hint and hope he'll get it. Men do much better when you directly communicate what you want.

Now that you've decoded some of the biggest mysteries of communicating with your husband, you're well on your way to becoming a husband whisperer! As a wholehearted wife, you may find that using

these tips to draw your husband into deeper heart-level communication will reap additional benefits in your marriage, including a more
loving relationship. They sure have worked for Erin and me!

With that in mind, let's explore the five levels of communication
in marriage.

Enhancing Communication in Your Marriage

As we stated earlier, communication is one of the most effective ways
to deepen intimacy in any relationship. On any given day, we communicate at various levels with different people. For example, you can
talk on the surface with someone—we often call that *small talk*—or
you can reveal your deepest needs and feelings.

*The small-talk of everyday life can be a genuine
road towards contact, a way of getting to
know somebody, a prelude to more profound
exchanges, a simple and natural approach.
But, let us admit it, it is also often used as a
means of avoiding personal contact. It is like a
prologue that goes on so long that the play never
begins. It allows us to be friendly and interesting
with people without touching on subjects that
would compel us to enter into real dialogue.*

—Paul Tournier, *The Meaning of Persons*

If you're longing for a more intimate, loving relationship with your
husband, you probably won't be satisfied with small talk or discussing
only the most superficial details of your life together. But each level of
communication plays an important role in a healthy marriage. Nurturing

heart-level communication in marriage requires an intentional investment of time and effort, but the depth and richness you can experience in your relationship as a result are well worth your investment.

Various relationship experts have examined numerous levels of communication, but we'll limit our discussion here to five basic levels.[9]

Level 1: Clichés. This is the most superficial level of communication. One common cliché exchange is "How are you doing?" followed by the typical non-communicative response, "Fine." At this level of communication, you never really learn anything about the other person, and you exchange essentially zero information. Healthy marital communication includes a little clichéd conversation here and there. Although this can be viewed as a common courtesy and can keep a positive tone in the basic interactions, couples who limit their conversation to clichés and can't think of deeper things to talk about with their spouses are in serious trouble. They may have reached a point in their marriage where they feel like total strangers living under the same roof. If this describes your marriage, don't despair. You have nowhere to go but up! If you need help relearning how to communicate with your spouse, we'd encourage you to seek out a professional Christian counselor. (Need help? Remember to call 1-800-A-Family for guidance in selecting a counselor.)

Level 2: Exchange of facts and information. This level of communication is a necessary and helpful part of life. Throughout the course of a day, we may need to exchange information to keep our schedules on track or to plan various activities. Some common examples of information sharing include . . .

"Did you see that it's supposed to snow today?"

"Hey, the highway looks like it's really backed up."

"The kids need to be picked up at seven from soccer practice."

Greg and I (Erin) are often communicating about these practical aspects of life, like getting the kids dropped off or seeing if there is anything needed from the store. It's very tactical, but also necessary for the day-in, day-out needs of our family. I'm sure you and your husband have these interactions as well. Families can't function effectively or efficiently without sharing information, but this level of communication has a major drawback: it doesn't build relationship. The intense pace and demands we face in marriage make it easy to live our lives at this level. Information sharing, though practical, is a very superficial way of communicating. If we're not careful, we can get so caught up in tactical communication that we never get around to anything deeper. When that happens, marriage can end up feeling like one long business meeting. To go deeper requires slowing down and taking the time to have a two-way conversation with our husbands.

Level 3: Sharing opinions. This level of communication is where we begin to get beyond the surface to what another person thinks. We might say things like . . .

"How can anyone vote for that person? He isn't trustworthy."

"I really like the coach for our son's team."

"Your sister is hard to get along with."

Sharing opinions falls into the arena where conflict can take place. We become a little more vulnerable when we express our opinions on various issues, and differing viewpoints can spark disagreements. So when we talk with our husbands at this level, we need to exercise tolerance and respect for their views, as well as a willingness to agree to disagree. We also need to listen with a desire to understand our husbands' viewpoints. Since there is more relational risk involved, we may sometimes choose to avoid sharing our opinions with our spouses. One sign of a healthy marriage is when husbands and wives are able to express differing opinions without a fear of being criticized or ridiculed. When we're able to listen and try to understand our spouses' perspectives on an issue, we build trust and intimacy in our marriages.

Level 4: Sharing feelings. At this level of communication, we open our hearts to our spouses and become much more vulnerable. We might share feelings like . . .

"What my father said on the phone last night really hurt me."

"When I walk in the door and am greeted with a list of demands, I feel unappreciated and unimportant as a person."

"I'm afraid because our finances seem really unstable."

Sharing feelings creates opportunities to be heard and understood. It's a doorway to growing in our relationships with our spouses and getting to know them better. In essence, this doorway leads to the hearts and souls of our spouses and gives us a glimpse of their true identities. Because of the risks for misunderstanding, hurt, and criticism, married couples sometimes avoid this level altogether, especially if they suspect it will only lead to conflict.

In a healthy marriage, feelings are respected and can be openly expressed based on a strong foundation of trust and intimacy that has grown over time. But couples also know when it's wise to keep their feelings to themselves until they can process them. If we can't share our feelings in appropriate ways with our spouses, then it's often best not to share them in that moment. If you are having difficulty feeling like its safe to share your feelings with your husband, you may want to pursue counseling to help establish some safe communication practices. Some simple techniques can be learned and applied with the help of a third party. It's worth the investment.

We also need to remember that our husbands may not feel as comfortable sharing their feelings as we do, so we need to encourage them in this area and avoid criticizing them when they do take the risk. For example, if your husband shares a feeling that offends you, don't react in a knee-jerk fashion by blasting him or shaming him. Instead, try to step back and understand where he's coming from before you respond.

Responding with three simple words, "help me understand," can let him know that you really do want to grasp what he is feeling.

Level 5: Sharing needs. This is the deepest level of communication because it requires the most vulnerability and trust in a relationship. Some examples of needs we might express are . . .

"I need some encouragement because I've been pretty beaten up at work today."

"I could use a listening ear because so much is swirling around in my head right now."

"I would love a hug."

You can also invite this kind of sharing by asking questions like . . .

"What do you need right now?"

"What can I do to encourage you?"

"It seems like you feel completely criticized and could use some understanding and moral support. Am I right?"

When we reach this level of intimacy in our marriage, we feel secure and accepted rather than judged as if we're on trial. We can trust that our husbands will hear us and understand the cries of our hearts in the needs we express. We believe they will honor our needs and do whatever they can to meet them (within reason, of course).

Expressing needs to our spouses isn't always easy, because we may fear that we'll be rejected or criticized. Or we may fear that our needs will be minimized or invalidated. If this has happened before, we may not feel safe sharing our needs and may need to rebuild trust before we're willing to risk being burned again.

Although expressing needs is often easier for women, it should go both ways in a healthy marriage. Your husband may not share his needs as readily as you do, but that doesn't mean he doesn't have any. One way you can encourage him to express his needs is to ask how you can pray for him during the day.

All five of these levels of communication characterize a healthy marriage. But so many marriages fall into the pattern of staying in the first two or three levels. If that's true in your marriage, make a point to pray about it and commit to taking steps of growth in this area. Just the fast pace of life alone, not to mention other factors that impact communication in a marriage, can keep us stuck at the more surface levels. Researchers found that the average American couple spends less than four minutes per day together, let alone talking at deep, heart-felt levels.[10] To improve this, be intentional. First, find a time that you both are available and typically open to deeper conversation. Some couples get up early in the morning and pray or have coffee together. Greg and I often take time after dinner—when everyone has food in their tummies. The kids can spend a few minutes playing or even cleaning up the dishes while he and I sit in front of the fireplace in the winter months or out on the back deck admiring the beauty of Pikes Peak in the summer. Knowing that this is "our time," we check in with each other and ask open-ended questions, trying to hear the emotions of the day. If we don't get to it after dinner, we will do this right before we go to sleep—committing to put our cell phones down—so we can listen well and pray for one another. It doesn't take a lot of time—but it has to be intentional time.

I can help you to accept and open yourself
mostly by accepting and revealing myself.

—John Powell, *Why Am I Afraid to Tell You Who I Am?*

If you want to reach the deepest levels of intimacy in your marriage, practicing the principles we presented in this chapter will help you get there. By becoming a better communicator yourself and nurturing your husband's communication skills, you can create an environment of refuge and comfort in your marriage. As you deepen the trust and security in your relationship, your husband may be more willing to let down his guard and open up. And you can show the way by being vulnerable with your own feelings and needs.

Asking questions and learning to share at deeper levels won't work if you treat them merely as techniques. True communication flows from a heart that is secure in Christ and filled with His love. That's why intimate communication in your marriage begins with your heart.

We'll discuss how you can develop that kind of heart in later chapters. But first we'll explore another kind of communication that takes place primarily in the bedroom.

◇◇◇◇◇◇◇◇◇◇◇◇◇◇◇◇◇◇◇◇ ♥ ♥ ♥ ◇◇◇◇◇◇◇◇◇◇◇◇◇◇◇◇◇◇◇◇

The Secrets of a Great Sex Life

I (Erin) met Kevin and Karen in a marriage counseling group not too long ago. They had done everything the "right" way before they married. As their dating relationship got serious, they committed to purity until marriage. And after getting engaged, they sought out premarital counseling.

When they walked down the aisle at Christmastime, they expected their newlywed bliss to last forever. But Karen got pregnant the first month of their marriage, and afterward life changed rather quickly. Shortly into the pregnancy, she was put on partial bed rest, and intimacy was "restricted" due to a low-lying placenta and preterm labor. These constraints immediately put a damper on Kevin and Karen's sex life. Their bliss faded unexpectedly.

Once their beautiful son, Grant, arrived, they assumed they would return to the level of intimacy they had enjoyed when they first married. But the nighttime feedings, a colicky baby, and a return to full-time work for both of them resulted in sex being shifted to the back burner. In a few years' time, they somehow managed to bring two more children into the world. Raising three active children consumed so much of their time and energy that their sex life became nothing but a distant memory.

By the time Kevin and Karen reached their tenth wedding anniversary, they felt a desperate need to get away alone. So Karen's mom flew in to keep the kids while Kevin and Karen took off for a romantic weekend celebration. They booked a suite at the nicest resort in town and planned a very special dinner for Saturday night. After arriving Friday night, they were exhausted and ended up just holding each other as they fell asleep. The thought of sleeping in was wonderful, and anticipation was building for Saturday night. It was going to be as special as their honeymoon!

After a lazy breakfast in bed the next morning, they did some quick Christmas shopping and enjoyed lunch at a local restaurant. In the middle of their lunch, however, Karen developed a migraine. She tried to ignore the pain and pretend it wasn't happening. How could she possibly be getting a migraine over their long-awaited weekend away? Soon the throbbing in her head was so bad, she couldn't avoid reality any longer.

Kevin drove them back to the hotel, closed all the blinds in the room, and tucked Karen into bed. Hours passed, but she didn't wake up. So Kevin canceled their dinner reservations and ordered room service instead, eating his meal while watching a football game. When Karen finally came to, she found her sweet husband holding her in his arms.

She later told me (Erin), "Although this wasn't the passionate, romantic weekend we envisioned, waking up in Kevin's arms made me fall in love all over again. It was so romantic because I knew that his expectations had been dashed." She went on to say, "I'm certain that this moment didn't mean the same thing to Kevin, but it sure did speak love to me. And believe me, I was much more motivated to speak love in his language after our special weekend away."

Like the twists and turns in Karen and Kevin's marriage, your marriage journey, including your sexual relationship, may not have turned out the way you expected. Children may have come earlier than you anticipated. You may have lost a parent shortly after you were married, experienced job loss, moved to a new location, or dealt with a significant health issue in the family. All of these stressors—along with many others—can negatively impact your marriage, especially your sexual relationship.

During my first year as a therapist, I (Erin) saw couple after couple who were dealing with concerns related to these types of stressors. I assumed that most of these couples would need counseling for financial issues, since I'd been told that money is typically the biggest conflict area in marriage. But the problem that actually triggered their decision to pursue therapy was a lack of satisfaction in their sexual relationship.

It seemed that no matter what was causing problems in the relationship, disconnection became very apparent in the bedroom. Complicating matters, couples found it difficult to have a healthy, productive conversation about their feelings, fears, and expectations regarding sex.

In this chapter we'll discuss ways you can improve your sexual relationship with your husband, but first we'll focus on what you can do to become a better sex partner. A great sex life starts with you!

Preparing Yourself to Connect Sexually

Let's face it, sex is complicated. Some women are dissatisfied with the extent of physical intimacy with their husbands and wonder, *Why doesn't he seem interested?* Others feel guilty because they often reject their husbands' sexual advancements or are reluctant to be affectionate, fearing that their husbands will interpret it as a sexual green light.

When women hear directives to "reserve some energy for your husband so you're not so tired when he wants you sexually," "initiate sex periodically," and "respond more often," it can feel as if their husbands are the only ones who matter and that wives are just objects for their husbands' enjoyment. Some women sense they're trying to feed an appetite in their husbands that never seems to be satiated. Others are frustrated trying to keep sex interesting or are discouraged because their sexual relationship is no longer satisfying personally. And a few just wish this part of their relationship would magically go away.

As a woman, I (Erin) want to be the wholehearted wife God is calling me to be and embrace the gift of a fulfilling sexual relationship that He has given Greg and me. I want to prioritize sex and maintain a vibrant connection with Greg, but the sexual dimensions of marriage are so multifaceted that at times I feel that making our sex lives vibrant is easier said than done. Sometimes I'm able to focus on this dimension well. At other times, when the demands of life are flooding me, I don't pursue sexual intimacy wholeheartedly—or maybe even at all. Most of us understand that passionate connection in marriage ebbs and flows. But I think many wives get stuck in the "ebbing" part, where sex seems passionless—like a marital discipline of sorts. We may find ourselves wondering, *What happened to the beautiful purpose for sex that God designed?*

Remember how Kevin responded to Karen's throbbing headache? He tucked her into bed, ordered room service, and then held his wife. An amazing husband, right? But obviously we can't control how our husbands will respond when it comes to sexual intimacy. Sometimes it will be "Kevin-like," and other times it may feel "Devil-like."

The central thread throughout this book is learning to control what we can and letting God deal with the rest. And we can control only ourselves. I always have a choice as to how I respond to Greg and how I show up for the sexual component of our marriage. Honestly, I don't want to feel as if sex is merely a duty or an obligation. I want to live out what Paul described in Ephesians 6:7: "Serve wholeheartedly, as if you were serving the Lord, not [people]." I believe that this is the greatest advice on finding sexual fulfillment—the decision to serve our husbands.

Sex is one of the ways we can serve each other in marriage. (It gives "outserving" each other a whole new meaning!) Serving is a choice I get to make. I can serve reluctantly or wholeheartedly. As I mentioned earlier in the book, being a *wholehearted* wife involves the whole person—emotionally, spiritually, mentally, and physically. The best way to serve wholeheartedly is to learn how to proactively prepare myself in these four areas. So let's talk about how we can serve our husbands sexually by nourishing our whole person.

Men and women differ in many ways, including gender characteristics, physical makeup, personality traits, and family and personal history. One of the most dramatic ways men and women differ is how they connect emotionally. Women typically have a greater desire to connect with their spouses emotionally. This emotional connection is critical for us to desire sexual intimacy. Our hearts need to be engaged before our bodies can respond physically. We want to feel loved and cherished, and we need to experience nonsexual displays of affection before connecting sexually with our husbands. This feeling of connectedness has come to be known as "emotional intercourse."[1]

With my body, I thee worship. My body will adore you, And your body alone will I cherish. I will with my body declare your worth.

—traditional wedding vow

Emotional intercourse involves connecting with each other on a heart level. More than likely, we'll be the ones driving this type of connection. If emotional intimacy is an essential need for us, we can't wait for our husbands to initiate it. We need to be proactive and find ways to get this important desire met. Figure out what emotional connection looks like for you and let your husband know what he can do to meet this need.

In general, emotional intercourse for women involves talking about feelings, sharing details of their day, touching non-sexually, making eye contact, expressing empathy and compassion, showing curiosity, revealing hopes and dreams, being complimented, spending time together, being served, receiving small gifts, and so on. Keep in mind that for most men, this type of connection isn't going to come naturally, and it's definitely not their default response. So, more than likely, you'll need to initiate emotional intercourse with your husband. Don't expect him to read your mind. Instead, proactively discuss with him what needs to happen first for you emotionally so that you're motivated and ready to connect with him sexually.

Preparing Your Soul for Sex

Praying together, talking about what God is teaching you, embracing the beauty of God's creation, and worshipping together comprise what we call "spiritual intercourse."[2] It happens when a couple connects intimately on a spiritual level. According to Nick Stinnett's worldwide research, one of the elements consistently found in healthy, loving families is shared, meaningful religious experiences.[3] If your husband is willing, ask him to spend some time discussing how you can best connect spiritually. Even if your husband doesn't share your faith in God, you can still embrace God's perspective on sex personally.

God has much to say about sex in His Word—much more, in fact, than just instructing us to "be fruitful and multiply" (Genesis 1:28, NASB). He wants us to *enjoy* sex. As author Ed Wheat points out, "God Himself invented sex for our delight. It was His gift to us—intended for pleasure."[4]

Think of God as the amazingly creative designer of sex! He planned sex as a unique and integral part of marriage—a celebration, not a burden. He could have just come up with a simple technical process for reproduction, but instead He conceived of sex—an amazingly intimate act intended not only for procreation but for great pleasure and a one-of-a-kind unity. Sex is an experience that deepens our marital bond and strengthens our connection with our husbands. It's also an area in which we can add creative flourish and flair to reflect our unique selves.

To prepare yourself spiritually for sex, meditate on the fact that God is the creator of this delightfully intimate physical aspect of marriage. Understanding God's design for sex and adopting His perspective are essential for connecting sexually with our husbands and embracing sex more passionately.

Preparing Your Mind for Sex

One important aspect of preparing our minds for sex is to understand that most women don't think about sex like men do. We've all heard the jokes about men having one-track minds. Well, there's definitely some truth buried beneath the jokes. Understand that your husband is very visually oriented. Even if he doesn't mean to think about sex, his mind will often drift that way when he notices a pretty woman. But you and I don't have these biological cues to remind us about sex the way men do.

As women, we have to be more intentional about lovemaking. Typically, our brains are overloaded with household and work responsibilities, relationships, our children, and even what to make for dinner. It's essential that we make room for thinking about sex. Linda Dillow, a speaker and writer on intimacy in marriage, talks about marking her calendar with "T. S." or "think sex."[5] This reminds her that sex is a priority and that preparing her mind for sex is beneficial for the entire experience. I actually began putting this into practice after I heard her speak about it.

One other way you can prepare your mind for sex is to become aware of what might be keeping you from responding sexually to your husband. Following are some of the roadblocks women may experience:

- Stress
- Fatigue
- Conflict in the marriage or other relationship issues
- Lack of non-sexual touch or other displays of affection
- Hormonal changes
- Distractions (small children, work, and household responsibilities)
- Past sexual abuse
- Depression or anxiety
- Use of certain medications, including birth control
- Previous sexual history
- Poor body image or lack of confidence
- Fear of getting pregnant
- Difficulty achieving orgasm or experiencing pain during intercourse
- Physical changes related to menopause

Take note of any areas on this list that are preventing you from connecting sexually with your husband. Pay particular attention to the areas you can control and deal with personally. You want to get rid of these roadblocks so that you can experience a more vibrant sexual relationship.

It's especially important for the sake of your heart and your marriage to get help if you have been a victim of sexual abuse. Seek out a Christian counselor who specializes in this area so that you can begin the healing process. If you've never explored the impact sexual abuse has had on your heart or the lies you may believe because of it, it's critical you do so. And if other issues on the list are negatively impacting your sexual relationship, don't hesitate to consult a medical professional or Christian counselor for help in resolving them. (I can't recommend counseling enough! If you need help finding a qualified guide, I'll remind you again to call Focus on the Family's counseling-referral network at 1-800-A-FAMILY.) Most of all, ask the Lord for His faithful guidance and care as you seek healing in these areas.

Understanding the differences in how you and your husband view sex and becoming aware of obstacles to connecting sexually and seeking help to resolve them are three of the most important ways to prepare your mind for connecting sexually. But even more important is remembering that God created each of you for sex in wonderfully unique ways. Spend time thinking about this and thanking Him for these differences.

Preparing Your Body for Sex

One of the biggest hindrances to our female libido is exhaustion. In *The Good Girl's Guide to Great Sex*, author Sheila Wray Gregoire states that "given the responses [of over one thousand women] to my survey about sex, I think more women have rotten sex lives because they're too tired than because their husbands are distant."[6]

In an online article, Gregoire described an all-too-common scenario:

> Little kids are hanging off of you. Or maybe you're running to
> the office where you have to deal with grumpy people. You're
> in a rush. The phone is ringing off the hook. You're just looking
> forward to the day ending when you can actually relax! . . .
> When we feel like everybody is hanging off of us and every-
> thing is on our plates, we're going to absolutely crave time to
> ourselves. And when do we take that time? When the kids are
> in bed—right when we could be enjoying [our] husband![7]

With life's demands, is getting in the mood for sex even realistic? I believe it is. But we have to do this intentionally. It won't happen unless we put sexual intimacy higher on our personal priority list. Yes, there are inevitable times life can squeeze out the opportunity. But for the sake of God's beautiful design and the health of our marriages, we don't have to act as if rare sex is an inevitable part of life. If you struggle with exhaustion and stress, make a plan to deal with it. Start by listing some activities that would refresh you and help you prepare physically for sex. It could be working out at the gym, walking with a neighbor, eating right, soaking in the tub, getting a massage, taking a nap, and listening to relaxing music.

As you prepare yourself for connecting sexually with your husband, remember that the most essential component is your soul. So make sure to include prayer and time in the Word in your daily routine. Also try to include activities that renew you spiritually, emotionally, and intellectually, such as reading a worthwhile book, joining a Bible study, having lunch with a girlfriend, scheduling coffee with a mentor, hiring a babysitter to give yourself personal time, journaling, scrapbooking, and so on. Whatever the activity, discover what fills your tank and pursue these things.

If you're rolling your eyes and thinking, *Sounds great, but I can't see it happening this side of heaven*, don't get discouraged. Pray. Ask God for ideas that are realistic for your season of life and honestly assess what is filling your days. Can you exchange something that's less important, such as watching television, for spending more time with the Lord and connecting sexually with your husband?

Talk with your husband and brainstorm ways to prioritize your sex life. I promise he'll find a way to watch the kids if it means you'll be more available in the bedroom! Otherwise, ask a family member to babysit or trade babysitting with a friend. Remember, taking great care of yourself is in the best interest of your sexual relationship. You can't give what you don't have.

God created sex for marriage, and we're the only ones who rightfully can give our husbands this gift. Keep in mind that there are times in marriage when we simply choose to give this gift even though we may not feel like it. Let's commit ourselves to doing everything in our power to keep the passion in our marriages alive. As we nurture all the ingredients of a great sex life, we'll move toward a more loving relationship with our husbands.

Connecting Sexually with Your Husband

As wholehearted wives who are committed to fulfilling our husbands sexually, we need to understand the important role sex plays in their lives, as well as what they need from us as sexual partners. Lots of men can relate to Robert Byrne's quote, "Anyone who believes that the way to a man's heart is through his stomach flunked geography."

There are plenty of pithy one-liners and jokes about the importance of sex to a man. But there's more to men than just sex. As you read through this section, realize that these are generalizations and that your husband might view sex differently. The point is to offer you a window into the mind of the average man when it comes to sex. Hopefully this will ignite a spark of curiosity within you to ask some great questions. I (Greg) encourage you to use the following information and perspective as a launching pad to better understand your husband. So let's jump right in and explore some of the things husbands wish their wives understood about their sexual needs and the role sex plays in their lives.

1. Understand our sex drive. Sure, you get that, in general, a woman's sex drive is lower than a man's, but most women completely underestimate how important sex is to their husbands. Dr. Juli Slattery, in her excellent book *No More Headaches*, says,

From the female perspective, male sexuality is often viewed as a sordid desire. It seems to represent the worst of masculinity—passion without love, drive without self-control, sensuality without sensitivity. I've talked to more than one wife who would rather pretend that her husband's sexuality just didn't exist. At best, women tend to compartmentalize their husbands' sexuality. Sex represents Mr. Hyde, tainting an otherwise moral and approachable Dr. Jekyll. . . . Over time, their sex life has become a burden. They feel guilty for withholding and responsible to keep their husbands pure, but mostly they wish the whole ordeal could just be put on hold for a couple of years.[8]

Yes, men have a bigger sex drive, but we're not dogs. The vast majority of husbands do not run around trying to sleep with every woman we see. We truly love you and are passionate about monogamy. Our fidelity matters to us, but so does sex.

2. We get "turned on" very quickly. Although you get aroused very gradually and need to warm up to the idea of sex, men don't have to have much foreplay, or even forethought, to be ready for sex. This is why my dad's classic line "Sexually, men are microwave ovens and women are Crock-pots" is so true. This is also why I love the joke about what women and men need to be ready for sexual intimacy:

For the woman: Support her, hold her, compliment her, listen to her, laugh with her, cry with her, romance her, encourage her, believe in her, cuddle with her, shop with her, give her jewelry, buy her flowers, write love letters to her, and go to the end of the earth and back again for her. Now she might be ready sexually!

For the man: Show up naked!

Your husband gets aroused very quickly because he's able to compartmentalize the sexual experience. He could have the worst day ever and still enjoy sex. Emotions can impact a man sexually, but at times he can push those aside and be instantly ready.

3. Sex is a legitimate physical need for a man. As a woman, you don't experience the physiological drive for sex or the need to "release" in the same way men do. For men, sex is an appetite that keeps returning. Here's what I mean. Sperm cells are building up 24/7, and simply put, they want out. If there isn't a release, your husband may find it uncomfortable or, in some instances, painful. To help you understand how this feels, think about when you have to urinate really badly or when a nursing mother's breasts are painfully engorged with milk. It is similar for a man. Relief will happen through ejaculation by orgasm, masturbation, or nocturnal emissions (wet dreams). But we would much rather it be with you! Understand that this urge to release sperm is how God made us, and it's a good thing for our relationship. As therapist David Bentley explains,

> [This need for sexual release] keeps us coming back to you again and again. It forces men to work through our differences with you and apologize when we're wrong or have acted selfishly. It reminds us to treat you well, to talk with you, to listen to your heart, to be romantic, and to help you.[9]

4. Realize that sex is intimacy to us. For most women, intimacy is primarily an emotional thing; for most men, it's primarily physical. Men can separate sex from a relationship, which might be difficult for you to understand because relationship and sex are so intertwined for women. Juli Slattery explains this difference well:

If you really want his attention, work with the way God designed him. . . . Your sexual relationship may be the "on-ramp" to communication, conflict resolution, and building the emotional intimacy you are longing for.[10]

Use your husband's God-given desire for *your* benefit as well. When you give him the physical intimacy he desires, it releases oxytocin (the bonding hormone), which significantly increases the chance that your husband will provide the emotional support you long for. Author Sharon Cohen agrees: "When I respect [my husband's] desire for sex—and not always by merely 'giving in' but by inviting, encouraging and enjoying it—my emotional needs are met."[11]

Use us—I promise, we don't mind!

5. *Understand that our sexuality is a core aspect of our identity.* In her best-selling book *For Women Only*, Shaunti Feldhahn explains that sex has a deep emotional impact on men. Her research revealed that sex dominates their expressed needs and desires. Shocking, right? However, the fascinating part of her study was the *emotional component* behind male sexuality. Most husbands indicated that being sexually fulfilled in marriage significantly impacted their confidence and masculinity. Seventy-seven percent of men agreed that if their wives were interested and motivated sex partners, it would give them "a greater sense of well-being and satisfaction with life."[12]

What does this mean for you as a wholehearted wife? Understand that as much as men want sex, we also hate rejection. When you don't pursue us sexually, seem to have little interest in sex (even for very legitimate reasons), or fend off our advances, right or wrong, we hear rejection. Your "Not tonight" translates into "I'm not interested in *you*."

Author Paul Byerley explains how sex is core to a man's identity:

For men sex is intimately connected with their sense of masculinity, self-image, and self-worth. I don't know if that's good
or bad, but I know it's a fact of life. This means sex is personal,
and that having sex makes him feel loved, appreciated, and valued, while not having sex makes him feel the opposite. Wives
often say "It's not personal" when saying no to sex. For her it's
not personal, but for him it is. Even if he can accept it's not personal for her, . . . it's still personal for him. "No" still hurts, it's
still a rejection, and it still makes him feel unloved, undesired,
and unneeded. [13]

Try to remember that when your husband pursues you sexually, if
you remain uninterested, it can impact him negatively on many levels.
Make sure that if you're responding with a no, you gently discuss it
with him. Men are more fragile emotionally than their wives often
realize.

Juli Slattery perfectly explains a husband's emotion around sex:
"You cannot compartmentalize your husband's sexuality. You cannot
love him as a husband but reject him sexually. From his perspective, his
sexuality is a central part of who he is as both a man and a husband."[14]

6. We need compliments as well. As women, you look in the mirror,
but so do we. Men also make negative judgments about how we look.
We can feel unattractive, out of shape, and embarrassed to let you see
us naked. These things make us question whether you still desire us
anymore. However, when you compliment us, this gives us sexual confidence. More importantly, as bodies change and age, remember that
the beauty of a person really is more than skin deep. Your husband can
become beautiful to you when you remind yourself that God created
the human body—*his* human body—in a unique way, amazing in all
of its functions and intricately and intentionally designed. See God's

glory in your husband as a total person, including the external packaging. And then verbalize that to him.

7. *We like it when you initiate sex.* Most husbands feel as though they're the ones who always initiate sex. But we also like to be pursued—especially sexually. It's nice to feel desired. We don't want you to have sex with us because you feel guilty. We want you to *want* to be with us. Don't be shy about letting your hubby know you're in the mood. Remember, "T. S." (think sex).[15]

8. *At the same time, don't take it personally when we don't initiate sex.* I (Greg) have said that men need sex. So what does it mean if your husband doesn't pursue you sexually or seems to have no interest in sex? This doesn't mean there's something wrong with you or that your husband doesn't want you. Don't jump right to personalizing this, second-guessing, or blaming yourself. Don't instantly conclude that he's having an affair or looking at pornography.

In spite of the myth that men want sex anytime anywhere, this isn't true. Men can compartmentalize various events (like a bad day at work), but they don't necessarily disengage from their deeper feelings. Although your husband might not be able to verbalize it, he cannot detach from what's going on emotionally.

As Dr. Dave Currie, former director of FamilyLife Canada, explains,

> In reality, a man's emotions can have a huge impact on his sexual desire. If he feels emotionally distant from his wife, and especially if he feels like a failure in any way, it can lead to a lack of confidence and therefore a lack of interest in sex. For a man, sexual performance is very much tied to ego, so if he is not feeling good about himself it will definitely show up in his approach to sexual intimacy with his wife.[16]

Realize that other issues—both physical and emotional—can affect your husband's sex drive. These could include stress and exhaustion, feelings of inadequacy, low testosterone levels, erectile dysfunction, or other factors. Yes, there are times where an unusually low interest in sex may be caused by pornography or drug or alcohol abuse. But if your husband lacks interest in sex, be wise and sensitive in conversing with him about it. Remind him that you love him and want your sexual connection to grow. With sensitivity and a teammate mentality, ask him if there is anything affecting his desire to be sexually intimate. Inquire about anything you're doing that might be impacting his sexual desire (nagging and complaining, criticizing, rejecting him, being controlling, etc.). Commit to stopping these negative behaviors and ask if there are positive things you can do to renew his sexual interest.

9. We like a good quest. In his book *Wild at Heart,* John Eldredge says that deep in the heart of every man is a longing to romance and win the affection of his bride.[17] Unfortunately, these days there are very few quests to pursue. Many men get their adventures from video games and their romance from porn. This is heartbreaking! But in a healthy marriage, sex can be the adventure we long for. It's amazing that God made us to *want* to pursue you and made you to want to be pursued.

Invite a good quest in your marriage. Allow your man to court and woo you! And respond when he does. Compel him to live out Proverbs 5:18–19 (NASB): "Rejoice in the wife of your youth. . . . Let her breasts satisfy you at all times; be exhilarated always with her love." The New International Version says, "May you ever be captivated by her love."

Help your husband enjoy the adventure of captivating you. Marriage is the right context for flirting with and alluring your man. A woman can't force her husband to pursue her, but she can sure flirt, tease, hint, entice, and reward him—and marriage is the right place for this to happen.

11. Help us battle against sexual temptation. It's important to recognize that men are faced with enormous temptation in our world today. We're more visually stimulated than you are as women; plus, the world is throwing half-naked women at us in every other commercial on television, on the Internet, or at the mall. More than likely, your husband has daily battles with some form of temptation. Realize that God brought you into his life as a helper (Genesis 2:18). You help your husband guard against temptation by regularly connecting with him sexually. This is what the apostle Paul meant when he wrote,

> The wife has no longer full rights over her own person but shares them with her husband. . . Do not cheat each other of normal sexual intercourse . . . or you will expose yourselves to the obvious temptation of the Devil. (1 Corinthians 7:4–5, Phillips)

Juli Slattery offers this encouragement to wives:

> Your husband depends on you to be his partner in his battle against sexual temptation. Although you aren't responsible for his actions, you are a key component in his victory. You're the only woman in the world whom your husband can look at sexually without compromising his integrity![18]

She also recognizes that wives have a powerful gift:

> You cannot compete with the raw sensuality dangled at men in our culture. You have neither the energy nor the physical attributes to look like a cover girl or a *Playboy* centerfold. Yet what you do have to offer your husband is far more profound. Fulfilling your husband sexually encompasses so much more than the

physical act. It means inviting his sexuality into your marriage, embracing all that he is, hopes, and desires. It includes wanting to fully understand him and welcoming the sexual appetite that expresses his masculinity. It involves striving with him through weakness and temptation and covering his fears and failures. No magazine, no coworker, no porn site can be this teammate and confidante for your husband. This is your place; this is your power; this is your gift. Unwrap it.[19]

What About Pornography and Sexual Addiction?

Our culture continually tempts men with sexual images. Unfortunately, this has not only led to an increase in sexual addictions and pornography, but it has also impacted sexual relationships among married couples. Juli Slattery was so burdened by this that she and Linda Dillow founded Authentic Intimacy, a ministry that helps women address intimacy issues in their marriages and restore sexual intimacy with their husbands.

According to Juli and Linda, married couples under thirty years of age are facing challenges that previous generations have never had to confront.[20] One significant issue this generation is facing is that men are becoming more passive and women are becoming more aggressive. Another issue many couples are experiencing is a role reversal in which the wife has a stronger sex drive than her husband. Sexual messages in the media have contributed to the problem, but pornography is by far the most significant factor.

Many men have been raised on porn and have become accustomed to the instant sexual gratification it provides. As a result, they often don't know how to have a real sexual relationships with their wives. Or they may not want to invest the effort in connecting sexually, since women take time to respond, and men can interpret this as failure. An addiction to pornography can have a devastating impact on marriage. It can also lead to sexual addiction and other problems.

If your spouse is spending time looking at pornography instead of connecting with you sexually, you may be feeling rejected and betrayed. Or if your husband is showing signs of sexual addiction,[21] you may feel confused and even repulsed. Dealing with pornography or sexual addiction in your marriage can be extremely painful, and we strongly encourage you to seek professional help to address these issues and find healing in your relationship. Look for a Christian counselor who has had previous experience working with couples in these areas. (Remember, if you need help finding a counselor, contact 1-800-A-FAMILY.) You can encourage your spouse to join you in therapy, but remember, you can deal only with what you can control—yourself. If your husband isn't willing to get help, don't let that stop you from seeking it.

The road to recovery isn't easy, but don't give up on your husband or despair! God knows all about the struggles both of you are experiencing. He is a God of healing and restoration, and even in the darkest and most hopeless of situations, He is powerful to save! Trust Him to heal your sexual relationship and restore the intimacy He intended for your marriage.

Connecting Sexually as a Couple

Did you know that your sex life serves as a barometer for the rest of your marriage? It's true. Your sex life is generally a mirror reflection of your marital relationship overall, as well as the level of intimacy you're experiencing in other areas. As I (Gary) have learned over the years, a healthy sexual connection with your spouse is critical to a healthy and more loving marital relationship. Decades of research on sex and marriage bear this out:

- Dr. Mark Schoen of the Sinclair Intimacy Institute states that "a good sex life is an important part of an individual's overall health. . . . People who have a good sex life tend to feel better [mentally and physically]."[22]

- "Couples who take time to cultivate and maintain healthy and satisfying sexual relations tend to be more connected with each other and do not suffer from depression, heart problems, and other health problems."[23]

- Married couples tend to have more sex than those who are single or dating. They also report more satisfying sex lives than unmarried people who are sexually active.[24]

- Researcher Denise Donnelly has found that couples who aren't having sex at least once a month are much more likely to have unhappy marriages that end in divorce—unless both partners are satisfied with the frequency of sex.[25]

The bottom line is that sex is important for our overall marital satisfaction and even influences our physical health. Typically, connecting sexually in marriage makes us feel vital, young, and closer to our spouses. In fact, the more sex we have, the happier we report our marriages to be.[26]

And yet sex is the one topic couples are reluctant to discuss. They either prefer to keep it private, or they just don't know how to talk about it. This is unfortunate because communication really is the key to keeping our sexual relationships strong.

Talking About Sex

We're constantly flooded with sexual messages and images in our culture, so you'd think we'd be pretty comfortable talking about it. But ironically the opposite is true. Even couples who have been married for years struggle to talk about their sexual relationship.

Why is sex so difficult to talk about? One reason is that when we think about making love, we feel very vulnerable. Sex involves sharing ourselves with our spouses at the deepest level of intimacy. And as we know all too well, this can leave us feeling hurt or rejected. Sex can also bring back painful memories from the past. Growing up, we may have received negative messages about sex that have influenced how we view it as adults.

Sex is such a sensitive issue that many couples are reluctant to talk because they're not sure how their spouse will react. Will talking about it cause a fight or create more distance and separation? We may even be reluctant to talk about it because we feel too embarrassed to express our sexual desires and needs. Again, the irony is that we can't seem to talk about it, and yet we're getting naked and doing it.

The truth is, a vibrant sexual relationship requires great communication. It's the key to connecting sexually. As a wholehearted wife, I (Erin) want to encourage you to pour your time and energy into talking with your husbands about your expectations, frustrations, problems, and fears, as well as your likes and dislikes. We women need to be able to share our deepest feelings and tackle sexual issues with our husbands. When we bury our feelings and ignore problem areas, we feel more distant and disconnected from our spouses.

If you've never spoken openly with your husband about sex or find it a difficult subject to talk about, here are some tips that can help:

1. Focus on being SAFE. Make it your goal to create an environment that feels like the safest place on earth to talk with your husband. Feeling emotionally safe enables us to open up and reveal who we really are. When we women feel safe with our spouses, we know they'll still love, accept, and value us, no matter what.

Heart-level communication requires tenderness, honesty, eye contact, curiosity, understanding, validation, and empathy. Nurturing these qualities in your relationship will create a safe environment for intimacy and passion in and out of the bedroom.

2. Reminisce about sex. A great habit to develop in your marriage is talking about old times, or reminiscing. Think back to your first sexual experience together; your honeymoon night; your favorite place for making love; your best kiss; the most spontaneous, most romantic time; and so on. Share these memories with your spouse. Talk about what made these experiences exciting and what you enjoyed about them. Focus on positive, nostalgic memories about your sex life. This can help you talk more openly about your overall sexual relationship.

3. Mentor your husband. Men want to be successful, especially in lovemaking. They want to please you, but sometimes they simply don't know how. Ignore the fact that men are usually horrible at asking for directions—on the road or in the bedroom! Men are creatures of habit, and once your husband discovers something that seems to please you, he'll stick with it until you tell him otherwise. So tell him what does and doesn't feel good these days. Your husband needs good directions from you—when, where, how; what rhythm, speed, touch, and all that. Give him cues like oohs and aahs when it's pleasurable. Gently move his hands where you want them. Your feedback, instruction, and explanations will heighten your man's intuition and your pleasure. The more you talk while you're making love, the more likely you'll talk about sex at other times as well.

4. Earn a PhD in your man. The Hebrew word for "sexual intercourse" is *yada* (yä·dah'), which means "to know."[27] Become a student of your husband and make a real effort to understand him sexually. Get "to know" him! Ask him what turns him on and what turns him off sexually. Here are some other great questions to ask him:

- How could our sex life become even better?
- Do you prefer more quickies or more drawn-out sex?
- Would our sex life be more fun for you if we had sex in various places or tried different positions?
- On a scale of 1 to 10, how strong is your sex drive? Is it increasing or diminishing?
- Given your current sex drive, how often would you like to have sex?
- Is there anything you find wrong, offensive, or distasteful sexually?
- Do you have a favorite sex position? Why is it your favorite?
- What do I do that gives you the most sexual pleasure?

No matter how long you've been married, don't assume you know what your husband likes and dislikes sexually or what gives him the most pleasure. Make it a point to ask him these questions regularly so you can stay current.

One word of caution: If your husband suggests something in the bedroom that you aren't comfortable with or aren't quite sure about—gray areas such as masturbation, costumes, or fantasies—you need to think and pray about it before agreeing. Juli Slattery encourages couples to ask the following questions to determine whether a sexual activity is glorifying to God and honorable:[28]

- Does God say no to whatever it is?
- Does it involve just you and your husband, or does it introduce anyone else into your covenant marriage relationship?

- Is it beneficial to both of you and to your marriage? Certain activities may be permissible, but are they edifying? First Corinthians 10:23–24 says, "'Everything is permissible'—but not everything is beneficial. 'Everything is permissible'—but not everything is constructive. Nobody should seek his own good, but the good of others."
- Is the behavior addictive?

5. *When you need to talk about your sex life, pick the right moment and keep it positive.* Assess both your mood and your husband's mood before jumping into a sex conversation. Don't try talking about sex after a bad day at work or as you're both climbing into bed exhausted at the end of a long day. You can't have a productive conversation when you're mentally and emotionally drained. One or both of you will most likely end up feeling defensive or hurt. It's also unwise to discuss frustrations or scrutinize performance when you're between the sheets! Right before or after sex is when people feel the most vulnerable.

◇◇◇◇◇◇◇◇◇◇◇◇◇◇◇◇◇◇◇◇◇◇◇ ♥♥♥ ◇◇◇◇◇◇◇◇◇◇◇◇◇◇◇◇◇◇◇◇◇◇◇

Billions of people have had sex. I am not sure how many have actually made love.

—Sheila Wray Gregoire, *The Good Girl's Guide to Great Sex*

◇◇◇◇◇◇◇◇◇◇◇◇◇◇◇◇◇◇◇◇◇◇◇ ♥♥♥ ◇◇◇◇◇◇◇◇◇◇◇◇◇◇◇◇◇◇◇◇◇◇◇

Make a point to keep your bedroom and, more important, your bed a refuge—a safe haven. This isn't the place to discuss unresolved aspects of your sexual relationship or your disappointments and frustrations. Instead, schedule a different time to talk and choose some other private place in the house, such as a comfy couch—or better yet, go for a walk. (Men love to talk side by side, not face-to-face.)

Here are a few tips that can help you share your concerns in a loving way:

- As you begin your conversation, try not to make your husband feel inadequate or defensive. Give him the benefit of the doubt and assume that he has your best interests (and pleasure) in mind. Instead of saying, "We need to talk about our mediocre sex life," say, "I know you value our sexual relationship, so I want to talk about how we can make it better."
- Use "I" statements so you don't sound as if you're accusing or belittling him. Instead of saying, "You always rush our foreplay," try, "I would like to move slower and have more touching before we have intercourse."
- Don't just articulate the problem; have a specific solution in mind. Use this opportunity to brainstorm ways to juggle schedules or to find better times for sex.
- If you have trouble talking through the issues, consider seeing a professional Christian therapist. (As noted earlier, call 1-800-A-FAMILY if you need help finding a counselor.)

Remember, talking about your sexual relationship is an ongoing conversation, not something to check off your to-do list!

We've covered a lot of ground in this chapter, but we hope you've gained some valuable insights about how God designed sex so that you and your husband can experience more joy and passion in your relationship. A great sex life is all about preparing to connect sexually, understanding and appreciating the unique way God made your husband, and communicating from the heart. The benefits of connecting in the bedroom will flow into other areas of your relationship as well. Let the fireworks begin!

Key Seven: Managing Conflict
in a Healthy Manner

◇◇◇×××××××××××××××××××× ♥ ♥ ♥ ××××××××××××××××××◇◇◇

A Doorway to Intimacy

Even though Greg and I (Erin) teach conflict-resolution skills to other couples, that doesn't mean we always apply them in our marriage. It's one thing to know what to do, but it's another thing entirely to do it—especially in the heat of the moment. Let's face it, we all blow it from time to time, and that's exactly what I did in a recent conflict with Greg.

Greg was out of town for several days when an issue about his work hours came to a head for me. I generally try to wait until he returns home to bring up anything we need to work through, so even though this issue had been building for more than a month, I waited.

When Greg arrived home on Friday morning, he went straight to work—and I waited again. Friday night we had an event to speak at, so the issues had to be pushed to the back burner yet again. But by Friday night at ten, the volcano began to spew. And by ten thirty, it was a full-blown eruption. Believe me, I know that Greg and I won't exactly have a healthy discussion when I erupt—especially after ten at night!

All I had wanted to do was let Greg know I felt as if I was carrying the weight of our family's needs alone because of the amount of time he'd been working lately. It seemed so simple to communicate that to him. But I was obviously feeling some deep emotions about it all, so I erupted, spewing my frustration and anger at Greg instead of calmly expressing my needs.

It was not a great way to begin. But the good news is that by noon on Saturday we were having a healthy conversation about the issue. In the end we gained a greater understanding of what we were each feeling and needing and were able to connect on a deeper level.

———————————— ♥ ♥ ♥ ————————————

Conflict is inevitable, but combat is optional.

—Max Lucado, *The Inspirational Bible*

———————————— ♥ ♥ ♥ ————————————

Conflict in marriage is inevitable, but most of us avoid it like the plague. Why? Because it's usually about as pleasant as the plague!

Something may really be bothering us, but we aren't sure whether to bring it up or let it lie. It's like the proverbial elephant in the room—we know the problem is there, but neither we nor our husbands will address it. Instead of sitting down and resolving the issue—which would take all of fifteen minutes—we put it off, playing various scenarios in our minds, rehearsing interactions, losing sleep over it, and wondering what caused the problem in the first place. This past weekend, a woman came up to me at a marriage seminar. Through her tears she said, "I've realized that I've been avoiding conflict my entire married life." She went on to explain that she has personally experienced the impact of this pattern—"a disconnected, unsatisfied marriage." The great news is that she recognized this and was ready to start making some baby steps down a different road toward healthy conflict.

Conflict generally occurs over issues that matter to us. It reveals our hearts and the hearts of our husbands and becomes a window through which we catch real glimpses of each other. But because the process is so uncomfortable, threatening, or painful, we tend to avoid it. Unfortunately, when we avoid conflict, we miss out on deeper intimacy and understanding in our marriages.

Have you ever avoided conflict in your marriage because you feared it might make things worse? Or perhaps you've tried to resolve a conflict but ended up in a war zone because you handled it poorly. Believe me, I (Erin) have been there. But when we learn to resolve conflict in a healthy way, it can lead to a more loving and intimate relationship with our spouses.

The kind of conflict we'll be talking about in this chapter has to do with common marital issues that prevent couples from reaching the deepest levels of intimacy and connection. If the conflict you're experiencing in your marriage results in abuse, you need to get away from the abusive environment to a place of safety before you try to address the issues in your relationship. (We also strongly encourage you to seek the counsel of a trained Christian counselor or call the National Domestic Violence Hotline at 800-799-7233.)

The frustrations and hurts we experience in marriage can lead us to conclude that nothing good ever comes from conflict. We may view it as an inevitable reality of married life that must be endured or avoided like the plague. But conflict can be a gift in disguise when we realize that it's actually a doorway to greater intimacy with our husbands.

A Doorway to Intimacy

Conflict may be unavoidable in marriage, but if we learn how to navigate it, it can become the doorway to deeper understanding and connection with our spouses. Conflict creates opportunities to become more aware of our husbands' feelings and needs as we honestly recognize our own. It also has a way of revealing what both spouses really care about and brings hidden or unexpressed issues out in the open. Even though we may not think of it this way, conflict truly can be a gift.

Just as we often perceive conflict in a negative light, we tend to think of confrontation the same way. But when it's done in a healthy way and for the right reasons, confrontation can make us aware of issues we need to resolve in our marriages, and it has the potential to open the door to intimacy, bringing us closer together. Confrontation doesn't have to equal fighting. It can facilitate healing discussion even when it's painful and makes us vulnerable. Healthy confrontation enables us to open up honestly, confess hurt or sin, seek understanding, or set boundaries with the goal of bringing greater growth and unity to our relationship. Confrontation becomes unhealthy when it consistently turns angry or abusive, damages self-esteem, destroys trust, limits growth, or makes us feel unsafe or afraid. To avoid these hazards, we need to learn a more loving way to resolve conflict with our spouses.[1]

The first step toward resolving issues in a healthy way is accepting responsibility for your role in marital conflict and understanding what pushes your buttons. Knowing what sets you off and why can help you avoid volcanic eruptions and knee-jerk responses that fan the flames of conflict instead of resolving it.

Learning Healthy Ways to Deal With Conflict: You First!

You've probably heard the expression "Don't push my buttons."[2] When we say that, we're referring to actions or words that irritate us or in some way touch a sensitive spot for us. We all tend to react negatively (often in anger or hurt) to certain behaviors that pour salt in our wounds or rub us the wrong way.

One of my (Erin's) friends told me she thought of herself as a patient person . . . until she had children. Then she found out they could push buttons she didn't know she had. Well, marriage can do the same thing. So recognizing what pushes your buttons is an important step toward healthy conflict resolution.

A button might be something as simple as a pet peeve—like when your husband leaves the top off the toothpaste tube. A button could trigger fear or signify that you're being forced into a role that doesn't fit your natural strengths. A button could also represent unmet expectations, an unfulfilled relational need, or an old wound.[3]

One of my buttons is when one of the kids or Greg sits on my unmade bed in the clothes they've been wearing all day. Dirt and germs from wherever they've been are transferred to the sheets I'm going to sleep between for eight hours. It doesn't happen often, but my family knows it drives me crazy. Just this past week, Taylor was home from college and discovered Annie snuggled in our bed in her pajamas. Taylor, who had arrived from the airport just hours before, lay down next to her little sis to have a nice chat. But when I walked in the room, all I could think was, "Yuk! Airport germs from hundreds of people are all over my clean sheets!" Even typing these words makes my heart pound a little.

When our buttons get pushed, deeper, more intense emotions are triggered. We may feel anger or hurt on the surface, but at the root of these feelings are emotions that reveal the real issues, such as feeling unloved, disrespected, rejected, worthless, or abandoned. It doesn't really matter what gets you riled up. The key is recognizing the root issue or cause.[4]

So when one of my children or Greg sits on my bed in dirty clothes and pushes my buttons, the deeper emotion for me is feeling disrespected. That's ultimately the root issue I need to recognize and address.

In *Fight Your Way to a Better Marriage*, I (Greg) identify deeper emotions that are often at the root of various conflicts:

- Arguments about money can push buttons like feeling insecure or controlled.
- Arguments about household chores might push buttons like feeling taken advantage of and misunderstood.
- Arguments about children may push buttons like feeling invalidated and helpless.

- Arguments about sex can push buttons like feeling rejected or inadequate.
- Arguments about work can push buttons like feeling unimportant or misportrayed.
- Arguments about leisure time and activities can push buttons like feeling disconnected and misjudged.
- Arguments about dealing with in-laws might push buttons like not feeling good enough or feeling disrespected.[5]

How to Identify Your Buttons

1. Think about a recent conflict or a negative or hurtful situation with your husband—something that left you feeling frustrated, hurt, or upset.
2. As you think about this conflict, pay special attention to these questions: How did you feel about yourself in the middle of the conflict or hurtful situation? The question is not merely "How did you feel?" (e.g., hurt, frustrated, angry, etc.), but rather, "When you felt hurt or frustrated, what was the deeper emotion at its root? Possible answers might be "criticized," "controlled," "undesirable," or "abandoned."[6]

When our buttons get pushed and we experience intense emotion, our hearts close. In other words, we get into self-protective, defensive mode, like a little roly-poly potato bug that has just been poked and curls into a ball.[7] When we're in a defensive mode, we may do things like blame each other, minimize what our spouses are saying, belittle our husbands, escalate the argument, get angry, "catastrophize" the situation, or act out in some unusual way. On the other hand, we may also show defensiveness by withdrawing, avoiding, disconnecting, stonewalling, isolating, trying to mind-read our husbands, withholding love and affection, or becoming passive-aggressive. All of these reactions indicate that we've closed off our hearts toward our spouses.

Healthy conflict can't occur when we're on the defensive with closed hearts. Before we can have a productive conversation that helps us move toward understanding each other and resolving our issues, we must first open our hearts.

Opening Your Heart

Conflict may be inevitable in marriage, but we don't have to resign ourselves to unhealthy patterns of dealing with it. By God's grace, we can change how we handle conflict in our marriages!

Learning to resolve conflict in a healthy way has been a huge area of growth for me (Erin). The biggest part of this lesson was dealing with my own heart. It helped that I recognized my buttons and became aware of the underlying beliefs that triggered them, but in the end I still didn't handle conflict in a healthy way. I knew I had some important heart-level work to do that didn't involve my husband.

One of Greg's and my favorite Scripture passages is from the Sermon on the Mount. We already looked at it in chapter 4, but it's worth a second look:

> How can you say to your brother, "Let me take the speck out of your eye," when all the time there is a plank in your own eye? You hypocrite, first take the plank out of your own eye, and then you will see clearly to remove the speck from your brother's eye. (Matthew 7:4–5)

Jesus' message in this passage is clear. Before we confront the sins of others, we need to deal with our own sin first. When we remove the planks from our own eyes and open our hearts, we can address the sin in our husbands' lives with humility and grace.

The following steps can help you open your heart whenever you sense it closing toward your husband in the heat of conflict:

1. Take a time-out. Proverbs 29:11 says, "A fool gives full vent to his anger, but a wise man keeps himself under control." If you find yourself in a toxic exchange with your husband, take a time-out to de-escalate the conflict and regain some emotional equilibrium. Let your husband know you need to step away for a time so you can come back later and discuss the issue in a more healthy way. This is a time to cool off and let the anger and frustration die down.

During your time-out, avoid ruminating over details of the conflict. We call these "distress-maintaining thoughts,"[8] such as *How could he have said that to me!* or *Who does he think he is?* Instead, focus on activities that will restore your perspective and calm your emotions. Spend time in prayer, go for a walk or run, clean, do laundry, or journal. Talk to a friend only if you can share how you feel without bashing your husband.

How long should your time-out last? Long enough for your heart to open again.

2. Identify what you're feeling. You can't manage your emotions or open your heart until you figure out exactly what you're feeling. Welcome your feelings—don't deny, stuff, minimize, or ignore them. A UCLA study found that simply saying "I am feeling . . ." changes brain activity and reduces the intensity of the emotion.[9] Identifying your emotions and putting them into words can actually help you calm down, so don't skip this step!

3. Discover the truth. When our hearts are closed, we lack insight, awareness, and perspective. The Evil One will often try to intensify negative beliefs about our spouses. We must fight these negative thoughts by going to God in prayer and asking Him to show us the truth about ourselves, our feelings, and our husbands. When we turn to God for help, He fills us with His love and enables us to see ourselves and our husbands through His eyes. (If you struggle with a pattern of negative self-talk or self-hate, you may need to run your thoughts by someone who is godly, wise, and biblically grounded.)

4. *Ask God to soften your heart.* There are times when our hearts may harden toward our husbands—particularly with recurring areas of conflict. That's why we need God's help to change our hearts. In the book of Ezekiel, God promised the Israelites that He would remove their hearts of stone and give them hearts of flesh. Listen to how the *New Living Translation* expresses it: "I will give you a new heart, and I will put a new spirit in you. I will take out your stony, stubborn heart and give you a tender, responsive heart" (Ezekiel 36:26).

God is the one who gives us new hearts. We can't perform heart surgery on ourselves. Only God can work this miracle! This is reflected throughout the psalms, from David's repentant cry in Psalm 51:10 (NASB)—"Create in me a clean heart, O God"—to his desperate plea in Psalm 86—"Give me an undivided heart, that I may fear your name" (verse 11). As God performs His amazing heart surgery in our lives, we can cooperate with Him by choosing not to intentionally harden our hearts (Hebrews 4:7).

Keep in mind that you may not always need to go through these four steps in a linear fashion. It may be that crying out to God in a simple prayer will open your heart. Or maybe walking through just a couple of the steps will help, such as taking a time-out and identifying your feelings. Once your heart has opened toward your husband, re-engage with him and seek to have a healthy, productive conversation to resolve your conflict.

An open heart is essential for healthy confrontation and, ultimately, a more intimate, loving relationship with our husbands.

Engaging in Healthy Conflict with Your Husband

Now that you've learned about your buttons and the importance of an open heart in resolving conflict, let's look at three principles that will help you understand your husband's buttons and how you can engage him in healthy conflict. Just the other day I (Erin) witnessed Greg's buttons getting pushed—thankfully I wasn't the one doing the pushing. I was standing in the kitchen and our daughter Murphy came in from soccer practice. She was exhausted and not feeling great. She and Greg exchanged a few words and I could immediately see Greg shut down. He snapped back at Murphy—and I knew for certain he was in reaction mode. Murphy left the kitchen and stormed up to her room. As difficult as it was, I remained silent—although I easily could have "helped" him recognize what was going on. But before I could figure out what to say, he was already on his way up the stairs to apologize to Murphy.

Our husbands have buttons, just like we do. Isn't it nice to know that we wives aren't the only ones that can push those buttons? Sometimes it's difficult in the moment to know what to do when your husband's buttons get pushed by you or someone else, so here are a few helpful tips:

1. Learn to identify his buttons. You know what pushes your buttons and why, and you may know what pushes your husband's buttons (especially if you enjoy pushing them just to bug him). But do you know *why* particular behaviors or words are hurtful or irritating to him?

To engage in healthy conflict, you need to spend some time observing your husband and learning to identify his buttons as well as the root issues behind them. This doesn't mean it's a good idea to push his buttons just to find out what they are! Resist the temptation to push his buttons for the fun of it or to get even or irritate him. At the same time, you don't need to tiptoe around his issues. Instead, seek to understand what triggers intense emotions for him. Sometimes, you might even accidentally or inadvertently push his buttons, but the good news is it's also his responsibility to discover, to understand, and to manage his own emotions and reactions.

If he's open to talking about his feelings, ask questions that might help him identify the root issues behind these emotions. For example, "When I slammed the door, how did that make you feel?" If he says that your actions made him feel angry, encourage him look for the deeper emotion at its root, such as feeling rejected or disrespected. It's best not to ask these kinds of questions in the heat of the moment. Wait for a less emotionally charged time and be wise in the way you approach the subject, knowing how sensitive you are about your own buttons. Then be prepared to listen without getting defensive.

2. Choose your battles. Don't go looking for a confrontation with your husband. Instead, thank God for the good things about him and then ask Him to help you identify *significant* offenses you and your husband need to work through.

Choosing our battles requires insight and discernment to distinguish between petty offenses we should overlook or deal with internally, and significant offenses that need to be addressed. For example, confronting your husband when he forgets to put down the toilet seat probably wouldn't qualify as a significant offense. But lying or irresponsible behavior would.

Colossians 3:13 (NLT) instructs us to "make allowance for each other's faults." Are there irritations or complaints about your husband that you could let go of because they are truly insignificant? Could you choose to accept certain traits or habits rather than confront them? "Love covers over a multitude of sins" (1 Peter 4:8), and God graciously forgives your shortcomings. Can you extend the same grace to your husband?

One of my (Erin's) friends was continually bugged by the fact that her husband let his dirty clothes lie on the floor in a heap. Initially, she nagged him. Then when that didn't work, she grew resentful. Finally, after some prayer and consideration, she decided she would ask once more for his cooperation in addressing the issue and then let it drop. She realized that it took thirty to sixty seconds out of her day to pick up his clothes, and she had the choice to be angry about it or accept it. In this instance, she decided to accept it. Interestingly, after a few months without pressure from his wife, he began to pick up his clothes. Now the only time she finds them lying around is when he has occasional long, late nights at the office.

The bottom line is that you need to honestly determine what you can live with and what you can't. If you find that you can't easily overlook one of his behaviors, then you need to broach the subject with your husband in a loving and constructive way.

3. *Establish healthy boundaries.* This means distinguishing which issues are yours to own and which are your husband's. It also means identifying legitimate and appropriate consequences to implement if he violates your boundaries. For example, if a conflict throws your husband into an angry tirade, you probably need to tell him that you will be leaving until he can respond more calmly. Then exit the room or, if necessary, the house.

If setting boundaries is difficult for you, we highly recommend the classic book on that topic by psychologists Henry Cloud and John Townsend titled *Boundaries in Marriage*. In particular, their chapter on conflict presents some helpful guidelines for dealing with six types of conflict in marriage.[10]

The steps we've outlined in this section are designed to help you engage in healthy conflict with your husband. As you gain insight into your husband's hot-button issues, wisely choose your battles, and set appropriate boundaries for confrontation, you may be pleasantly surprised to find that conflict and confrontation in your marriage can actually draw you closer together as a couple. Even if you don't always agree, working through conflict in healthy ways can help you and your husband reach a win-win solution that benefits both of you. We'll explore this in more depth in the next section.

Resolving Conflict in Your Marriage

As I sat down to write this morning, I texted about ten close friends, telling them I was writing a chapter on conflict and would love to hear their stories on recent disagreements with their spouses. One text came back quickly with the reply, "Where do I begin?" Others reported disagreements over finances, distribution of chores, and situations with their children.

Their responses mirrored some of the common causes for marital conflict:[11]

- Money
- Sex
- Work
- Children
- Housework

Regardless of what you and your husband are arguing about, we believe that all marital conflict is rooted in one of these five underlying issues:[12]

1. *Power and control.* These issues often reveal themselves in arguments over finances, plans, or preferences. Examples include conflict over how money is spent, what to do over the weekend, or what movie to watch. Disharmony and conflict are inevitable when both spouses are attempting to gain control in some area or when one spouse is trying to prevent the other from taking control. This is when sparks fly in a marriage!

2. *Lack of respect.* Conflict also occurs when there's a lack of respect for key differences in gender, personality, or individuality. One or both spouses may feel that their feelings, decisions, or rights don't matter in the relationship. Or one spouse may show a lack of respect by trying to manipulate or change his or her mate. This is sure to cause a clash.

3. *Distance.* When one spouse is unavailable physically or emotionally to the other, disharmony is likely. Distance is also a way to protect ourselves from hurt. Sometimes one spouse will put up emotional walls for self-protection. Walls shut out the other spouse, creating feelings of rejection and abandonment, which often lead to conflict.

4. *Distrust.* Conflict thrives in an environment of distrust. When a relationship no longer feels emotionally safe, distrust and suspicion can build. One or both spouses may no longer feel comfortable expressing their feelings or needs in the relationship—perhaps as a result of lies or betrayal.

5. *Unmet Needs.* Conflict can erupt when one or both spouses believe that a need isn't being met by the other. An unmet need may revolve around time, money, attention, empathy, communication, or love. When these needs are ignored, minimized, or neglected in a marriage, resentment and hurt can build up over time and eventually lead to conflict. This may happen intentionally or inadvertently. Regardless of the cause, conflict can erupt slowly or spontaneously. For some reason, crazy and rushed school and work mornings are the perfect combination for conflict to erupt between members of our family. On this particular day, it was between Greg and me (Erin). Greg has a daily call-in radio program called *Everyday Relationships,* and on Mondays I get the opportunity to do the program with him. As we were all rushing around,

attempting to get out of the door, I asked Greg, "Hey, where did you put my prep sheet for the radio program?" He quickly shot back, "I have to not only prepare it but now deliver it to you too?" I was stunned at his sharp reaction. However, what I didn't realize was that Greg had been resenting the fact that I had been leaving all the prep work up to him. After I sought to understand what was going on, he explained that this felt unfair to him and that he had a need that was going unmet—for me to jump in and help. The great news is that I caught a glimpse into Greg's heart that morning. Although the insight came painfully at first, ultimately I was left with understanding my husband's needs a little better.

Any kingdom divided against itself is laid waste;
and a house divided against itself falls.

—Luke 11:17, NASB

Think of the conflicts that occur most frequently in your marriage. What underlying issues are at the heart of those conflicts? If you can begin to identify and discuss these issues, you and your husband stand a much better chance of resolving conflicts that arise in your marriage.

It would also be helpful if you and your husband create a list of rules for fighting fair. (A counselor may be able to help you do this in a single session if you need some objective input.) Here are some of the ground rules we suggest to couples:

- *Clarify and define your issue or topic.* Stick to the topic at hand and try to explain it clearly. Don't bring up ten other issues at the same time. Keep it simple so you can work toward a resolution on the issue that's most significant to you or to him.

- *Take responsibility for your feelings and actions.* Use "I" state-ments when expressing your concerns. For instance, instead of saying, "You're always late, and it throws off our family dinner," you could say, "I'd really like us to eat together as a family, but I feel frustrated when you get home later than you said you would."
- *Be direct and honest.* As we mentioned earlier in the book, men don't pick up subtle hints, so address issues as clearly and directly as you can. This does not mean that you can express issues in a rude, harsh, scathing, aggressive manner. What this means is being assertive with what is going on for you—being direct, but loving and kind. Always think of what will give you the greatest chance of being heard—a harsh word or a kind, direct statement?
- *Consider other factors that may negatively impact your ability to fight fair.* For example, if either of you is tired, hungry, stressed, or busy, you probably should table the discussion until those factors are dealt with. As we (Greg and Erin) travel together to speak, we have to be very careful to not jump on "opportuni-ties" to engage in conflict. We are usually very tired—we get up early (typically around four a.m.) on the first travel day to leave home; we arrive in our seminar city and begin teaching that night; the next morning we are usually dealing with at least a two-hour time change. We've learned to play praise and worship music in our room to battle the sleepiness that pro-duces grumpiness, and we table any issues that are pending. We have to protect this time—so we are unified as we step out to minister. You'll need to decide when to wait because of your own circumstances.
- *No discussions after 10:00 p.m.* This is a general rule we've decided upon that relates to the point above. (And actually,

as we've gotten older, it's usually nine p.m.) By the end of the day, most of us are too exhausted to discuss serious issues with our spouses. It's better to wait until you and your spouse have had a decent night's sleep; otherwise, one or both of you may blow a gasket! Healthy conflict resolution is worth waiting for. The verse "don't let the sun go down on your anger" isn't saying to work all your issues out before you go to bed. Therefore, we have learned to set many conflicts aside until morning—making sure that our individual hearts are open toward each other. Keep in mind that the wholehearted wife focuses first on her own heart!

- *Listen and share.* We must make an intentional effort to understand our spouse's side of the issue. Try to listen without interrupting as he shares his perceptions—and avoid the temptation to prepare your retort while he's speaking. I (Erin) know how difficult this can be. I often believe that I have the perfect thing to say to help him! But, listening involves giving him my ears, and not my mouth. Next, as you are listening, clarify anything you don't understand by asking questions or restating what you believe you heard. Once he feels understood, ask him if he would be willing to listen as you share your feelings and perceptions. It's amazing how much of communication can be miscommunication. Reflecting, repeating, and clarifying are great tools to avoid this.

- *Give your spouse equal time.* As a verbal processor I (Erin) talk to think. Often I end up dominating the conversation because I have an excess of words, or I cut Greg off as he is sharing. Instead, give your husband the opportunity to express his concerns and feelings first, and if he seems reluctant to talk, ask some questions to draw him out. Often going deeper with questions is easier for us as women—not always, but typically.

So come alongside of him by asking questions to gain understanding and giving him plenty of time to share.

• *Attack the issue, not the person.* No name calling or losing your
temper. If this happens, tell your husband you need to take a
time-out from the conversation and then review the steps we
presented earlier in the chapter for opening your heart. Ask
God to fill you with His love and help you see your husband
through His eyes. This can be a game changer! If your heart is
closed, we promise you that the conversation will ultimately not
lead to a deeper connection but probably cause further damage.

• *Paraphrase what you think you heard your husband saying.*
Reflect back to him what he told you. Clarify his words and
make sure you understand his feelings and perspective. Be
willing to give your husband the benefit of the doubt and
graciously acknowledge that you may not have heard him
correctly. Sometimes, especially after being married for many
years, you can begin to assume you know exactly what your
husband means or feels. It is so helpful to give him the benefit
of the doubt and ask for clarification.

• *Go forth as equals and teammates, seeking win-win solutions
to your conflicts.* Greg and I (Erin) have a "no-losers policy,"
which means that we recognize we're on the same team, and as
teammates, we win or lose together. We've learned to hear and
respect each other's concerns and convictions as we've worked
through conflicts. Over the years we've faced many conflicts in
the process of making major decisions, such as moving across
the country, adopting a special-needs toddler in our forties, and
choosing what video games we allow our son to play. In each
conflict we've tried to follow this policy. We state it this way: *It
is no longer acceptable for one of us to walk away feeling as if he or
she lost. We will find solutions that feel good to both of us.*

The most important ground rule for fighting fair is the last one: remember that your husband is your teammate for life, and knowing that, if you're willing to work together, you can always find a win-win solution for the conflicts you encounter.

Greg and I (Erin) use these five simple steps to find win-win solutions for our conflicts:[13]

1. Verbalize your mutual desire for a win-win solution.
2. Discover the "win" for each person.
3. Seek the Lord's opinion.
4. Brainstorm different solutions.
5. Pick a solution that feels great to both of you and put it into action.

Since we started following these steps, we haven't run into a conflict yet that we haven't been able to turn into a win-win situation!

We've shared a lot of information in this chapter, perhaps more than you can digest or put into practice all at once. So focus on at least one nugget of truth or suggestion that's most relevant to your marriage and start applying it to the conflict situations you and your husband encounter. There are some basic guidelines for dealing with the disagreements that will happen in this very intimate relationship called marriage. Take heart, even if working through conflict in your marriage doesn't always go perfectly. The way we (Greg and Erin) look at it is "we now know how to clean it up." Early on, as we have said, we were experts at getting into conflict, but clueless when it came to cleaning it up and getting to a deeper, more intimate place. We didn't realize at the time that we were missing out on drawing closer and experiencing a more loving relationship. As your sister wholehearted wife, I don't want you to miss out on this same gift of closeness that conflict can lead to in your marriage. Keep pressing forward until you reach the doorway of intimacy with your husband!

◇◇◇◇◇◇◇◇◇◇◇◇◇◇◇◇◇◇◇ ♥ ♥ ♥ ◇◇◇◇◇◇◇◇◇◇◇◇◇◇◇◇◇◇◇

Taming Volcanoes

It was one of those days. You know, the kind of day when everyone has something they need from you, and your calendar looks like a parking lot the week of Christmas. I (Erin) had taken all three kids to school and arrived late to a Christmas brunch that one of the Focus on the Family executive wives was hosting. After an enjoyable time, I hurried to my car because I was running late again, this time to a lunch meeting for work.

As I sped down the freeway, I reminded myself to slow down so I wouldn't get a ticket or skid on the snow-packed roads. Greg knew I'd be late, so by the time I arrived at the restaurant, he had already placed my order for me. After lunch we both rushed back to Focus headquarters for another meeting.

During that meeting I was never asked to share my opinion, and although I was sure it was unintentional, it still pushed my buttons.

I was a little fired up when I left, and I tried to soothe myself as I rushed to pick up our fifteen-year-old daughter, Murphy, from school. When I arrived at the high school, I was still irritated, which only added to my usual annoyance with the insanely crowded pickup lines at the entrance. Unable to find a spot to wait for Murphy, I sort of scrunched in between two lines until she finally arrived.

When Murphy got in the car, I quickly discovered that she'd also had a bad day, which seems to be a frequent occurrence for fifteen-year-old girls. I tried to make small talk, but that didn't go over very well. So as usual I dropped her off at home before heading to the elementary school to pick up Garrison.

As Murphy got out of the car, we had one more sarcastic interaction, and I drove away thinking, *What a perfect addition to this completely crazy, exhausting day. I can't even be a good mother today!* After that exchange, I was even more irritated and distracted than before, so I wasn't exactly paying attention when I hit a patch of ice in the neighborhood roundabout. The car started to slide, and I knew this was going to end badly. Ironically I realized that the out-of-control feeling I was experiencing reflected my life most days. But that profound insight ended abruptly when my car jumped the curb and slammed into a light pole. Could a day get any worse?

Apparently, yes. Just as I thought I'd hit rock bottom (or in this case, a big pole), the ten-foot-high iron light pole teetered and fell as if in slow motion. The light fixture at the top smashed into the ground, and glass shattered everywhere. My body was trembling as my mind tried to process what I should do. I quickly decided that I should take care of the next item on my to-do list. So I backed up the car and then headed down the street to pick up my fifth-grade son. As I drove I held back the dam of tears I knew was about to burst.

Then another thought struck me: *I should probably call someone and report that I hit a light pole.* But I had no idea whom to call. I wanted to call my mother, but I haven't discovered the direct line to heaven in the past six years since she passed away. So I called 9-1-1. I knew better. My mother was a 9-1-1 operator in Phoenix, Arizona, for more than twenty years. She would have been appalled that I didn't have the nonemergency number stored in my phone. I can still hear her voice: "Don't call this number unless you have a true emergency. Don't take a line from someone else who is having a heart attack."

As it turned out, I called the right place. The 9-1-1 operator asked me a few questions and then explained that since I had called voluntarily, I wouldn't be charged with a hit-and-run accident. I felt like a criminal. First I left a crime scene, as she described it, and now I was turning myself in for a hit-and-run. This day was getting better by the second!

After informing me that a hit-and-run would have put more points on my license than a DUI, the 9-1-1 operator said I needed to meet a police officer back at the "crime scene." *Perfect ending to a rotten day!* I thought.

I dutifully headed back to the roundabout and contemplated the terrible day I was having while I waited for the police to arrive. Soon the flashing lights of a cruiser rounded the corner. The officer was incredibly kind and didn't issue me a ticket even though he said I deserved one for destroying public property. I wanted to reply, "Just add it to the list," but I bit my tongue and managed to be respectful.

When I finally reached the safety of my home, I trudged up the stairs to my bed and crawled under the covers. Then the dam broke as hot tears streamed down the sides of my face. A day of frantic rushing and angry irritation had ended with the destruction of public property. I never imagined that my anger and irritation could have such costly results.

An Unacceptable Emotion

Have you ever had a day like this? Let's be perfectly honest: Women get angry too. Even wholehearted wives! But in our society, expressing anger often seems inappropriate for women, even though some seem to think it's more acceptable for men. As one researcher observed,

Anger in men is often viewed as "masculine"—it is seen as "manly" when men engage in fistfights or act their anger out physically. [But] for girls, acting out in that way is not encouraged. Women usually get the message that anger is unpleasant and unfeminine.[1]

If expressing anger is considered "unpleasant and unfeminine," how do most of us handle it? We ignore it, deny it, stuff it, take it out on our loved ones, stew over it, soothe it with comfort food—anything but express it in healthy ways. Anger often seems to be an unspoken emotion for women. But let's set the record straight. Anger is a normal human emotion that men and women alike experience every day. But as women, many of us have bought into the myth that anger is forbidden. Consequently, we understand very little about it or how to deal with it in ourselves or our marriages.

Anger is common in any marriage, but if you or your husband expresses it in hurtful or unhealthy ways, it can become a major obstacle to experiencing a more loving and intimate relationship. The key is learning how to understand anger and deal with it in healthier ways.

At this point you may be thinking, *How can I deal with anger in my marriage if I can't even handle it in my own life?* The good news is that help is on the way! In this chapter we'll not only discuss what anger is, but we'll examine the root issues that fuel it and explore some healthy ways to defuse it. When you learn how to recognize and deal with your own anger, you'll be much better equipped to defuse it in your marriage.

Understanding Your Anger

We all feel anger, regardless of gender. However, according to Drs. H. Norman Wright and Gary J. Oliver, certain triggers and underlying causes may be more common for women than men:[2]

- Abandonment
- Being a people pleaser
- Dealing with children, teenagers, and in-laws
- Discrimination for being women
- Disrespect
- Entitlement of men
- Feeling insecure around people
- Feeling sorry for ourselves
- Getting older
- Having to wait
- Lack of affection from our spouses
- Not dealing with previous anger
- Not enough quiet time for ourselves
- Not having our feelings valued
- Overcommitment
- PMS
- People talking behind our backs
- Selfish demands
- Stress

This list helped me (Erin) identify the factors that trigger frustration, irritation, and anger in my life—which include stress, children and teenagers, PMS, not having enough time alone, and getting older. It has also been enormously validating to realize that there are underlying reasons for my feelings.

What are your triggers? Think about it.

- Your toddler throws himself on the ground and has a temper tantrum while you're trying to hurry through the grocery store.
- The washing machine breaks right when you get back from vacation with suitcases full of dirty clothes.
- Your best friend tells you she won't be able to watch your kids tomorrow while you go to the dentist.

- Your husband doesn't tell you about a business trip in two weeks that conflicts with the surprise get-away you planned.
- You can't find your keys, and your kids are late for school— three days in a row.
- The bank calls to let you know that your checking account is overdrawn.
- You can't find the file you need for a meeting at work that starts in five minutes.
- Your teenager violates her curfew, and you wait up hours past your bedtime.

The list could go on and on. But the point is, each and every day we experience things that leave us feeling irritated and angry. Yet all too often we're unsure how to express it in a healthy way. Learning how to manage anger is important, but first we need to understand what it is and the role it plays in our relationships.

After working with couples for many years, I (Gary) frequently addressed the issue of anger in their marriages. When you are dealing with human relationships, it's an emotion you really can't ignore. In my book *Making Love Last Forever*, I described it this way:

Anger is an emotion. Like all of our emotion, there's nothing wrong with it in and of itself. It's our human response to something that occurs, or at least to our perception of that occurrence. In fact, some anger is good; we *should* get angry when we see an injustice or when someone is trying to violate our personal property lines. In such cases, our anger is what motivates us to take appropriate action. But after anger motivates us to do something good, we can't afford to let it linger inside us. We have to get it out. Anger is a good emotion when it gets us moving, but if we let it take root, we set ourselves up for a great deal of potential harm.[3]

It may be a relief to know that anger has a purpose and can be used for good when it's expressed in a healthy, constructive manner. Anger isn't the problem; it's the mismanagement of anger that wreaks havoc in our relationships. The biblical command says, "In your anger do not sin" (Ephesians 4:26). Notice that feeling anger isn't sin. Anger becomes sinful only if we allow it to influence our actions in sinful ways. The key is what we do with our anger.

It's perfectly normal and healthy to acknowledge that we're feeling angry. In fact, Christian psychiatrist Ross Campbell says that denying anger will simply channel it into passive-aggressive responses, which are more problematic over the long haul than dealing with anger honestly and openly.[4]

Before we explore healthy ways to defuse anger, let's discuss two important facts about the emotion itself:

1. *Anger is a secondary emotion, not a primary feeling.* It generally disguises other emotions and often occurs after we've felt fear, frustration, hurt, or some combination of these three emotions.[5] And sometimes anger is triggered by an unfulfilled expectation that causes us to feel disappointed.

When you experience anger or you encounter someone who is angry, try to remember that there is likely more to the picture. Sometimes it's easier to feel compassion for ourselves or others when we realize that fear, frustration, or hurt is hidden underneath smoldering anger. This doesn't give us, or anyone else, the right to explode in anger or rage at someone. But recognizing that anger is often a secondary reaction to inner fear or hurt can help us respond to angry people, including our spouses, with understanding and compassion.

In every scenario we encounter, we have a choice: We can recognize that our emotions are normal responses to everyday occurrences, or we can ignore our emotions or stuff them. When we mismanage our anger, we risk destroying relationships—especially with those we love the most.

2. Anger can be buried. Just as anger camouflages other emotions that are hidden beneath the surface, it can also be buried alive. We can pretend it isn't there anymore, but it will resurface when we least expect it. And eventually it takes root in our hearts.

As we mentioned earlier, denying anger usually leads to passive-aggressive behavior. We're still angry, but instead of acknowledging it and verbalizing the issue, we end up behaving in covert ways, trying indirectly to get back at the person we're angry with. For example, you might just happen to forget to drop off your husband's pants at the dry cleaners even though you know he needs them for a trip this weekend. Passive-aggressive anger typically leads to resistant, unhelpful behavior like this.

Buried anger can also cause anxiety and depression, as well as a host of other physical problems, including headaches, digestive problems, heart problems, and high blood pressure. It can interfere with relationships, thinking, and behavior as well.[6]

For years I (Gary) have used the metaphor of "knotting up inside" to describe what we do with anger. That happens to be just the opposite of the word *forgiveness*, which means "letting loose" or untying the knots. When we get angry and stay angry for a long period of time, it's like creating tangled knots inside our hearts. Over time the knots can grow, bundle up, and get stored in what I like to describe as an "anger can."[7] We accumulate anger internally like compressed air in a can. Then when we brush up against someone or something that causes us to feel one of the three primary emotions (fear, frustration, or hurt), we let it rip. It's just like a can of Silly String. We push the spray button, and it unloads a gooey substance on the target of our anger. Whomever we've unloaded on is left feeling as if they've been sprayed with goo!

Remember, anger isn't the problem; it all depends on how we

handle it. When we handle it poorly, we push away those we love the most, leaving a trail of damaged relationships in our wake. Ultimately, unhealthy ways of dealing with anger can be passed from one generation to the next, causing even more destruction. But when we deal with anger in healthy ways, it can lead to greater understanding and intimacy in our marriages.

I (Erin) can remember my father raging when I was a little girl. It was terrifying at times. He was usually such a gentle man, but when he became angry, watch out! In response to those experiences, I always said, "I'll never be like that!" I'm guessing some of you have also made pledges just like this.

Legacy of a Dominating Dad
Drs. H. Norman Wright and Gary J. Oliver

Daughters of dominating, angry fathers develop a firm determination to live their lives in a way exactly opposite to what their fathers believed or stood for. They think that in so doing they will show their fathers that they won't be controlled. But what their angry, negative reaction really shows is that these women are still being controlled by their fathers. No wonder their anger doesn't recede.

Sometimes a father controls by becoming demandingly dependent on his daughter. He exaggerates his need to control his daughter, and the daughter becomes increasingly angry at him. Eventually she makes herself less available to be used, but now her guilt directs the anger back against herself.[8]

I swore I would never marry a man who raged, thinking this would take care of any issues I had with unhealthy expressions of anger. However, I quickly became aware of the many opportunities marriage gave me to become angry. (Can anyone say "Amen"?)

I can still remember Greg's face the first time we got into a major disagreement, and I started raising my voice at him. He looked dumbfounded and dazed—almost confused. I screamed my next words and then waited patiently for him to scream back, but it didn't happen. I remember thinking, *What's wrong with him?*

Soon I learned that Greg came from a family that never expressed anger by yelling. He actually came from a family on the opposite end of the spectrum—they typically denied their anger. So he wasn't quite sure what to do with my outbursts. But it didn't take long to "train" him to engage with me. Amazingly, when we spray our spouses with our anger, they often begin to display the same behavior.

Passive-aggressive behavior is the most immature way of handling anger. The most mature ways of handling anger are verbally, pleasantly, and resolving anger toward the person at whom we are angry if at all possible.

—Dr. Ross Campbell, *How to Really Love Your Child*

I never really shared this with anyone while it was going on because of the shame and guilt. I felt horrible after I'd throw a fit. I just knew that God desired more for me and my family. So I prayed for the Lord to heal me and help me learn how to handle my emotions when I got angry.

My struggle with anger drove Greg and me to learn more about how to better manage conflict in our marriage. When I realized that anger was a secondary emotion—masking fear, hurt, or frustration—I tried to put a name to what I was feeling when I became angry. I also learned that anger is a behavior—a reaction to feeling these primary emotions. No one "makes" us angry. We *choose* to react in anger when these underlying emotions are triggered.

As I cried out to the Lord for help with my anger, He began to work in my heart and life. I'll never forget the day I began to yell at some poor soul in my home, and nothing came out. As a matter of fact, I began coughing. It actually hurt! I was coughing—and rejoicing—all in the same breath. I believe that God heard my desperate cries—my heart's desire to break this pattern in our family. And to this day, I can't scream without coughing or hurting my throat. When I do blow it, I return to the injured party with an open heart and seek forgiveness. I often say something like, "I'm so sorry! I blew it! It is not okay for me to talk to you like that. It's really unacceptable. Will you forgive me?"

We all experience feelings of anger toward our spouses, and many of us either spray it at them or deny its existence. The key issue isn't whether or not we get angry but what we do with it.

Breaking Free from a Legacy of Anger

In my own struggles with anger, I (Erin) learned that I couldn't break the cycle without help. The unhealthy patterns I learned as a child were so deeply ingrained in my soul that I felt powerless to change them. I realized that only the Lord could bring about the heart-level changes I so desperately needed. And as I cried out to the Lord, He began to set me free from this legacy of anger.

Without the Lord's help, I couldn't overcome the ingrained pattern of anger I learned as a child. In the midst of your own struggles with anger, cry out to the Lord for His help and healing touch. Ask Him to give you an accurate understanding of what is really going on and to reveal the underlying issues that are fueling your anger, including unhealthy patterns you may have learned as a child. Then seek out a godly woman for accountability—or get professional help, if needed.

Of all the legacies our families of origin can leave us with, anger is one of the most toxic. If you're struggling with anger and rage, it's likely that one or more family members did too. The truth is, many of us didn't have great role models growing up. That's why understanding your family history is an important first step in breaking free from this legacy. When you become aware of unhealthy patterns in your family of origin, you can avoid repeating them.

In *Taking Out Your Emotional Trash*, Georgia Shaffer notes six destructive ways of expressing anger that you may have learned in your family of origin:[9]

1. *Acting out aggressively.* This aggressive, outward expression of our feelings may involve shoving, hitting, kicking, throwing things, or breaking items. We may also be verbally aggressive, engaging in yelling, name-calling, insults, or cursing.

2. *Speaking critical words.* Criticism involves finding fault with another person or expressing disapproval. Verbal attacks and being critical may seem similar, but criticism isn't always as obvious. When delivered politely without using a loud voice or foul language, criticism can be very subtle. If we're experienced criticizers, we may deliver our verbal jabs while smiling and saying, "I'm only telling you this for your own good."

3. *Engaging in vengeful behavior.* When we feel hurt, the desire to get back at someone can be expressed by our actions. When we focus on getting even, our unresolved anger and hostility can take root in our hearts and grow quickly into bitterness.

4. *Making sarcastic remarks.* Sarcasm is characterized by biting comments that are intended to inflict pain. If we grew

up in a sarcastic family, we may have enjoyed embarrassing and hurting others. When others are hurt, we may tell them they're being too sensitive and defend ourselves by saying, "I didn't mean anything by it. Can't you just take a joke?"

5. *Withdrawing communication.* This pattern of behavior is known as the silent treatment. If others offend us, we may avoid communicating with them. We may refuse to answer emails, text messages, or phone calls for days, weeks, or even years. When we inflict the silent treatment on others, nothing ends up getting worked out, and our anger often gets buried.

6. *Withholding something a loved one needs.* This destructive behavior involves holding back the very thing we know someone wants or needs, such as our love, time, attention, sex, money, or other resources.

Do you recognize any of these destructive patterns in yourself or your marriage? These behaviors create an environment of hostility, distrust, and discord. Toxic anger feeds our fears and insecurities and shatters our peace. Instead of leading to the intimacy and connection we're longing for in our marriages, it drives us apart and, in the end, destroys our relationships.

By contrast, we can begin to break these destructive patterns by learning some healthy and appropriate ways to express our anger:

1. *Take a time-out.* As we talked about in the previous chapter, taking a time-out is essential when we realize we're engaging in unhealthy behaviors. A time-out allows us to get away from the stressors that are fueling our anger so we can gain perspective and begin to calm down. Take a walk, breathe deeply, talk to God, talk to a friend, listen to praise and worship music, write a letter, vacuum, or do whatever helps you let off steam.

2. *Identify why you're angry.* What triggered your anger? A hurtful conversation, a frustrating situation, or some unnamed fear? Contemplate the underlying emotions that ignited your anger and name them. Often a current situation can trigger feelings from the past, perhaps from your childhood. Considering these factors will enable you to gain perspective and give the physical symptoms of anger time to diminish.

3. *Evaluate the basis for your anger.* Are you angry because you didn't get your own way? Do you need to confess selfishness or ask forgiveness for hurting your spouse? Are you angry because you experienced an injustice that needs to be confronted? Regardless of what caused your anger, pray first about how you should respond.

4. *Consider ways to deal with the cause of your anger.* After you've identified the cause of your anger and the underlying emotions, make a plan of action to address the issue. List your options and try to envision the outcome of each. Try to understand your spouse's point of view. How could you express your anger calmly and appropriately? What sort of win-win solution could you and your husband negotiate together?

5. *Get help if you need it.* Talking to a professional Christian counselor or a godly, older mentor can help you sort things out and decide the best way to express your anger and address the cause.

Understanding the underlying issues that trigger our anger and learning healthier ways of expressing it can help us begin to break the unhealthy patterns we brought into our marriages. No matter how deeply ingrained those patterns may be, God is able to root them out of our lives as we cry out to Him for help. If we allow Him to change us, He can heal our relationships and enable us to build a legacy of peace and love.

Dealing with Your Husband's Anger

Living with an angry husband is like living at the base of an active volcano. It can keep us in a constant state of hyper-vigilance—always on the alert, anticipating the next eruption. Even a small emotional outburst can cause us to fight back, freeze up, or shut down. Here's how one wife described her experience with an angry spouse:

> My husband has an explosive temper. Every few months, he'll go into a screaming rage, and it scares me. When he is de-pressed it's more frequent. It's always over something small and insignificant. . . . He will yell at the top of his lungs, swear at me, and intimidate me into backing down. Just the look . . . on his face is enough to completely freak me out. . . . It's like he's a different person when he gets angry. . . .
>
> We both realized recently that [his anger] has broken my spirit. . . . [I'm] afraid of setting off his temper, so [I'm] con-stantly walking on eggshells. . . . We . . . both agreed that I shouldn't have to live that way anymore. . . . Obviously fighting back when he loses his temper is pointless, so we decided that [I should] walk away when he starts getting ugly. We agreed that I don't have to let him talk to me that way, and that [we] can . . . continue the discussion when he's cooled down.[10]

As this woman discovered, dealing with anger is never easy. Thankfully most of us usually experience only minor eruptions when our husbands snap at us under stress or when they've had a bad day at work. But if the men we promised to love, honor, and cherish spew molten lava at us on a regular basis, it can be terrifying—especially if a normally godly man transforms into a monster.

As we mentioned earlier, anger is a normal emotion. It becomes a problem only if we or our husbands handle it in unhealthy ways. So how can we, as wholehearted wives, defuse our husbands' anger and encourage them to deal with it in healthier ways? Here are some guidelines:

1. Never accept responsibility for your husband's anger. We don't "make" our spouses angry. They choose to react in anger because our words or behavior triggered some deeper emotion or issue. That doesn't mean we don't need to accept responsibility for our own words and actions. But we are never to blame for their anger or how they express it. This is entirely their responsibility. They can choose to talk about their hurt or frustration in a healthy manner, or they can lose their temper, lashing out in hurtful ways.

James 1:19–20 tells us that "everyone should be quick to listen, slow to speak and slow to become angry, for man's anger does not bring about the righteous life that God desires." Each of us is accountable to God for how we handle our anger. We can either allow our sinful natures to control us, which leads to "fits of rage," or we can be controlled by the Holy Spirit, which leads to peace and self-control (Galatians 5:20, 22–23). We can't make this choice for our husbands. Like us, they must make this choice in every situation.

2. Set effective boundaries. An effective boundary enables us to take care of ourselves in a way that also strengthens our relationships with our husbands. (If you need a refresher on how to nurture yourself, review the suggestions in chapter 2.) We should never use boundaries to erect walls around our hearts or sever our relationships with our husbands.

The critical question to ask when establishing a boundary is, "What do I want to accomplish?" The ultimate goal is to "create a safe space that enables [our hearts] to remain open to God, self, and others," including our husbands.[11] A Christlike boundary will always draw us toward our husbands rather than driving a wedge between us.

It's important to set a boundary when your husband allows his temper to get out of control. You might say something like, "I would love to better understand what's bothering you, but if you choose to yell or threaten me, I'm going to walk away. I'll return when you're willing to speak in a way that honors both of us." You must then be prepared to follow through. Whenever you set a boundary like this, realize that it can take about twenty minutes for the adrenaline to diminish enough so your husband can engage in a healthy conversation.

Make a clean break with all cutting, backbiting, profane talk. Be gentle with one another, sensitive. Forgive one another as quickly and thoroughly as God in Christ forgave you.

—Ephesians 4:31–32, *The Message*

3. Try to understand why your husband gets angry. Seeking to understand behavior is an aspect of empathy, but that doesn't mean you should accept blame or responsibility for your husband's hurtful behavior. Empathy isn't about enabling your husband's anger; it's about keeping your heart open. Understanding the reasons behind your husband's behavior can keep your heart from hardening toward him. It can also help you pray for him with greater insight and compassion. As we discussed earlier, look for the underlying emotions behind his anger—fear, frustration, or hurt—and lovingly address those issues together.

4. Love the man; hate the sin. Your husband needs to know that you love him and are still his teammate, even though you disagree with the way he is choosing to express his anger. Keep in mind that if your husband is struggling with anger, he probably inherited that legacy from his family of origin. Ask God to help you see your husband through

His eyes. Pray for your husband and encourage him to turn to God for help and healing. Only God can break the sinful patterns in his life and help him learn healthier ways to deal with his anger.

If you ever feel physically unsafe, and your husband's anger crosses the line into physical slaps, pushes, shaking, or shoving—get help immediately. Call the authorities or seek safety at a safe house. It's never okay for your husband to rage, scream, throw things, threaten you, or hit you. If anger is a serious issue in your marriage, we strongly encourage you to seek Christian counseling. (Call 1-800-A-FAMILY for help finding a counselor with expertise in this area.) If your husband refuses to go with you, don't let that stop you from getting the help and support you need.

5. *Forgive your husband for his hurtful reactions.* I (Erin) learned the importance of forgiveness when we brought our adopted daughter, Annie, home from China. Greg and I had read about the grief reactions children can have when they're torn away from caregivers they've grown close to. Annie was no exception. She loved her nanny, Rose, dearly, and at first she reacted with a lot of anger toward me. It was one of the most painful things I've ever experienced. I had prayed for this child for over a year and had saved a lot of money to adopt her, only to be repaid with head butts, slaps, shoves, and pinches. It was horrible. But a very wise friend had given me some solid biblical advice before we left for China: "Erin, forgive Annie anytime she does something that hurts you during the time of transition. Say out loud, 'I forgive you, Annie!' "

Little did my friend know how desperately I would need that advice. It helped me keep my heart open toward Annie each time she pushed me away or had a temper tantrum. I am so thankful I forgave her, because after three weeks of pushing me away, she suddenly changed her tune one day and let me in. Tears streamed down my face as my heart overflowed with joy.

Looking back, I realize how very important it was to forgive Annie along the way. It wasn't okay for her to strike out at me, so I had to set boundaries and enforce time-outs to let her know that her behavior was unacceptable. I also discovered that the lesson I learned with Annie applied to my marriage. Next to my relationship with the Lord, the most intimate relationship I have on earth is with Greg. But Greg is human, and he can say or do things that hurt my feelings, sometimes without even realizing it. And at times he gets angry with me and may not handle it well. No matter how Greg behaves, my job is to love him wholeheartedly, setting appropriate boundaries and always being willing to forgive.

We (Erin, Greg, and Gary) hope these guidelines will enable you to keep your heart open toward your husband regardless of the way he deals with his anger. Ultimately, he is responsible for his anger, but you can play an important role in encouraging him to express it in healthy ways.

Defusing Anger in Your Marriage

As we've already discussed, marriage is a unique relationship. The depth of love and intimacy we experience with our spouses exposes us to a much wider range of emotions than we tend to experience in other human relationships. In fact, dependency and vulnerability in marriage are as likely to lead to hostility as they are to affection.[12] Dr. David Mace observes that "marriage and family living generate in normal people more anger than [they] experience in any other social situation."[13]

We learned in the previous chapter that conflict is the doorway to intimacy. But mishandled anger is often a roadblock to the deeper connection we desire with our husbands. Many couples say that expressing angry feelings is uncomfortable, and they actually try to avoid it. But remember that expressing anger in a healthy way doesn't mean you're being aggressive; it actually means you're being assertive. Assertiveness protects our relationships and allows us to value both ourselves and our spouses. Sharing our feelings about concerns or issues, even if it involves frustration or anger, is always in the best interests of our relationships with our spouses.

Unresolved anger can have a detrimental effect on any relationship, especially intimate relationships like marriage. That's why the Bible tells us not to let the sun go down while we're still angry (Ephesians 4:26). The reason is clear. When we don't work through our anger, Satan gains a foothold in our lives and can use it to drive us apart (verse 27). And as we discussed earlier, when anger goes unchecked, it can become buried, causing resentment to take root and harden our hearts toward each other. This happened in Karen and Ben's marriage:

> One night Karen awoke from a dead sleep. The wind was howling outside and tossing the outdoor patio furniture back and forth. Suddenly she realized that two of the tables had glass tops that could break, and just about then she heard a loud shatter. She tried to awaken her husband, Ben, but he said sleepily, "What does it matter at this point? They're probably all broken. Let's deal with it in the morning." Then he rolled back over and dozed off.
>
> Karen was seething as she went outside to haul the patio furniture into the garage. She resented that Ben was inside, snuggled warmly in bed, while she was in the dark doing hard labor at 4:00 a.m.
>
> "Boy, will I let him have it in the morning!" she said through clenched teeth.
>
> If this had been the first time something like this had happened, Karen might have been willing to give Ben more grace. But it seemed lately as if many household responsibilities were falling on Karen's shoulders, and she was constantly trying to coerce Ben to help her. She felt like such a nag. *If only Ben*

would respond to my requests, she told herself, *I wouldn't nag or be so angry all the time.* She even prayed that God would motivate him to help more around the house.

From Ben's perspective, he was already helping out a lot at home, but all Karen noticed was what he didn't do. It didn't seem to matter that Ben had been carrying extra weight at work after his boss was let go. In fact, he was sick and tired of shouldering the weight at work and at home. But when he tried to explain this to Karen, she would often get stuck in a rage and throw temper tantrums. *If she would quit nagging and screaming,* Ben thought, *I might be willing to help her more.*

Ben dreaded coming home in the evenings after work now, and yet it was so stressful at work, he didn't want to stay there either. So day after day he would come home bracing for the next onslaught of criticism. The distance continued to build between Karen and Ben, and neither could see the other's perspective.

Short-term anger is common in marriage, but letting offenses and hurt feelings drag on for months and even years not only damages our relationships; it can be fatal![14] Anger has the power to tear our relationships apart and push us away from each other. Much like Karen and Ben, ongoing resentment and anger can leave a couple feeling like there's a Grand Canyon of distance between them. Unresolved anger can cause us to become more cautious, mistrusting, and fearful of relationships, not only with our spouses but also with God. That's why it's so important to honestly acknowledge our anger, learn to express it in healthy ways, and encourage our husbands to do the same. If we want more loving relationships with our spouses, we need to defuse the ticking time bomb called anger!

Key Nine: Forgiving

◇◇◇◇◇◇◇◇◇◇◇◇ ♥ ♥ ♥ ◇◇◇◇◇◇◇◇◇◇◇◇

Set the Prisoners Free

On January 18, 2013, *USA Today* posed this question: "CAN YOU FORGIVE LANCE ARMSTRONG?[1] After years of vigorous denial, seven-time Tour de France champion Lance Armstrong finally confessed that he had used performance-enhancing drugs. Americans were stunned. Many fans who had been greatly inspired by his cycling successes and cancer recovery felt extremely let down.

According to Frank Farley, former president of the American Psychological Association, "America is the land of second chances. All you have to do is ask [for forgiveness]—especially if you can throw a ball, sing a song, make a speech, coach a team or hold the camera."[2] The article noted other public figures who have been forgiven—Michael Vick, Martha Stewart, and Bill Clinton, to name a few—and laid out a four-step plan for "fallen stars" who want to be forgiven for their sins and indiscretions:

1. Confession: "I did it."
2. Contrition: "I'm sorry I did it."
3. Conversion: "I will not do it again."
4. Atonement: "I will [make it right]."[3]

Interestingly, these four steps contain words that have significant spiritual meaning. The article illustrated an important truth about forgiveness in any relationship. When sin is uncovered, it brings us to a crisis point. How do we move forward? Can we ever forgive the offender? What are the consequences if we refuse, and what happens if we grant forgiveness, even if it isn't genuinely sought?

While the sins of public figures may never affect us, the sins and failings of our spouses can have a monumental impact on our lives. What we do at these crisis points in our marriages is what really matters.

In such an intimate relationship as marriage, it's almost impossible not to step on each other's emotional toes. As we discussed earlier in the book, intimacy naturally invites conflict and hurt feelings. We can't truly love another human being unless we're willing to embrace pain with pleasure.

><><><><><><><><><><><><><><   ♥ ♥ ♥   ><><><><><><><><><><><><><><

It flies in the face of all your pride, . . .
It's the whisper in your ear saying, "Set it free."
Forgiveness.

—Matthew West, "Forgiveness"

><><><><><><><><><><><><><><   ♥ ♥ ♥   ><><><><><><><><><><><><><><

The hurts we experience in marriage are often more than minor bumps and bruises resulting from short-lived tiffs or differences of opinion. As we soon discover, the greater the intimacy, the more likely we are to experience deep personal offenses that cause a crisis of forgiveness. Intimacy creates an environment that forces us to decide whether we will forgive and let go of the offense or harbor a grudge. It also challenges us to humbly ask our husbands to forgive us when we step on their emotional toes. Without forgiveness, intimacy and love wither and die. But when we learn to forgive, setting ourselves and others free from offenses, these qualities thrive in our relationships.

Our oldest daughter, Taylor, learned a valuable lesson about forgiveness during her sophomore year in high school. Her English teacher gave the class a very interesting assignment: to write a letter of apology to someone in their life whom they had hurt—a friend, a family member, a teacher, or a coach. Taylor took the assignment to heart and wrote a letter to her younger sister, Murphy. Murphy was in the sixth grade at the time, and as we all know, sixth grade is a rather awkward stage of life for most girls, so the letter couldn't have come at a better time.

Taylor was heading to Memphis with her youth group for a missions trip over spring break, so she instructed us to give Murphy the letter to read during our vacation flight to New York City. Murphy was sitting in the row right behind us, and I'll never forget the look on her face as she began reading. At first the glimmer of a tear ran down her cheek, and then she began shaking with emotion.

Here's what the letter said:

Dear Murphy,

I hope you have a great time on your trip with Mom, Dad, and Garrison. I'm sad that I won't be with you, but I knew I needed to go on this missions trip. A few weeks ago my English teacher gave us an assignment to write a letter of apology to someone we have hurt, and I immediately knew I was supposed to write you.

Murphy, over the years we have had our challenges. We have had our fair share of fights; however, we have had many fun times as well. I have become very aware that I haven't always treated you like you deserved to be treated. I have been cruel with my words and actions. I have called you names and fought with you over things that really didn't matter. Today I want you to know that *you matter* much more than anything else. I am deeply sorry for how I have treated you, and I am wondering if you might be willing to forgive me. I know that our relationship can be very different, and I hope that this will mark the beginning of a new chapter as sisters.

I love you with all my heart!

Taylor

Wow! With a humble, repentant heart, Taylor broke down emotional walls that had built up over the years and changed her relationship with her sister forever. That's the power of forgiveness!

Forgiveness Is a Choice

As Taylor learned from this assignment, forgiveness is a choice. She could have written a letter of apology to anyone, but she chose to ask Murphy to forgive her. As a result, they have become best friends. What a valuable lesson to learn so early in life!

Like Taylor, we can initiate a journey of forgiveness in our marriages. The choice is up to us. Our marriages may have sustained only minor damage from occasional offenses, disappointments, and unmet expectations. Or we may have deep scars from years of back-and-forth verbal pummeling and mistreatment. Over time our hearts can become so hardened from the wounds we inflict on each other that forgiveness can seem impossible. Even if we truly want to forgive our husbands for unresolved offenses, we may stubbornly insist that they should make the first move toward reconciliation. Our husbands often feel the same way, which leaves us in a deadlock.

The truth is, if we desire a more loving relationship with our spouses, as wholehearted wives, we must learn to keep short accounts and forgive on a regular basis. Rather than dwelling on our husbands' hurtful words and actions, we need to follow Jesus' advice in Matthew 7:5: "First take the plank out of your own eye, and then you will see clearly to remove the speck from your brother's eye." By taking the planks out of our own eyes, we can influence the overall condition of our relationships. Reconciliation and healing won't take place overnight, but forgiving can be a critical turning point in our relationships.

Forgiveness communicates to our spouses that we value them, and it can soften our hardened hearts toward each other. It doesn't erase what has happened, stop the pain, or magically heal the wounds, but it allows our relationships to move toward deeper levels of intimacy.

Forgiveness starts when we make the decision to forgive, regardless of whether our emotions necessarily line up with our decision. In other words, we can *choose* to forgive even when we don't feel like it.

As believers, we're commanded to forgive just as God has forgiven us (Colossians 3:13). It isn't always easy—but then again, forgiving us cost Jesus His life! Remember His amazing words as He hung on the cross: "Father, forgive them, for they do not know what they are doing" (Luke 23:34). Jesus is our perfect role model. He chose not only to forgive those who nailed Him to the cross but to experience the cross in the first place, so that we could receive eternal forgiveness. If for no other reason, we need to forgive our spouses out of gratitude for what Jesus did for us.

When it comes to love, we can't give what we haven't experienced ourselves. The same is true of forgiveness. If we haven't grasped our desperate need for God's forgiveness, we aren't able to truly forgive our husbands—or anyone else—when they sin against us. My (Erin's) dear friend Carrie Oliver said it like this in *Grown-Up Girlfriends*: "Before we can forgive others, we must embrace God's forgiveness of our weaknesses and our sins."[4]

Forgiveness is not only a choice and a command; it's also a process. Our society tends to demand instant gratification. We want things immediately. But forgiveness doesn't work like that. Depending on the gravity and magnitude of the offense, it can take weeks, months, or years—or even a lifetime. But regardless of how long it takes, the decision to forgive is always worth it.

When we choose to begin the journey of forgiveness, we're often the ones who receive the greatest benefit. We can finally stop playing the tapes in our minds that continually rehash every offense and, instead, push the eject button.[5] The wounds may still hurt for some time, but as we continue turning to the Lord for help, we can stop reliving the offenses. For a while we may have to choose forgiveness on a daily basis, reminding ourselves of the decision we made until God heals our wounded hearts. In some ways, the process of forgiveness is a decision to "redecide" every day. But by God's grace we can keep making that decision again and again.

The choice to forgive is a powerful gift that can transform relationships. It applies not only to forgiving our husbands but to forgiving ourselves as well. This is often where we need to begin.

Forgiving Yourself

We can all think of poor choices, mistakes, or circumstances we've made in the past that we wish weren't part of our history. It's like something lurking behind a closet door in a dark hallway. Quite frankly, we would prefer to deadbolt the door and forget about the painful, shame-filled memories it conceals. No one else may know these events ever happened, but we certainly do. We may try desperately to keep others from discovering our secret sins, but when we avoid them, they exercise immense power over our thoughts and behavior. Guilt and condemnation can wrap their tentacles around our hearts, filling us with self-hatred. No matter how hard we try, we can't forget what's lurking in the closet, and we can't forgive ourselves for the things we've done. All too often their power to destroy our relationships is much greater than we realize.

The past can catch up with us just as it caught up with Eileen. On a Thursday morning, Eileen cheerfully answered the phone. But the joy rapidly drained from her face and heart when a female voice said, "This is a very important private phone call. Please do not hang up. Does March 11, 1968, mean anything to you?"

Eileen's heart began to pound and her hands trembled as she responded, "Yes, yes it does."

"Did you have a baby on that day?" A baby girl?" the woman asked.

After several moments of dead silence, Eileen finally responded, "Yes, yes I did."

Then she heard the words she had always dreaded: "Well, I am that baby."

Eileen never thought her daughter would find her. A few years earlier, Catholic Family Services informed her that the daughter she had given up for adoption was requesting to contact her. Eileen immediately declined the request. No one knew about her baby girl. Not her other daughter, who was three years old when Eileen gave up the baby for adoption. Not even the husband she'd married eighteen years later, or her seven stepchildren. This was a secret Eileen had tried to lock away for a lifetime. And now on the phone was her youngest daughter. Eileen panicked. Did this girl not realize the damage her phone call could do? At the very least, it had reopened a painful wound in Eileen's life.

Experiences like Eileen's can leave our hearts deeply wounded and scarred. Many of us have secrets we want to lock away in dark closets forever. Perhaps you had premarital sex that left you feeling like a failure for not waiting until marriage. Or you may be carrying hidden guilt and grief from having an abortion as a young woman. Maybe you became addicted to drugs or alcohol at an early age. Or perhaps you've struggled with an eating disorder, an addiction to pornography, or been on the receiving end of someone's maltreatment that left you feeling unlovable or deeply ashamed.

Whatever our past experiences may have been, if we deny or ignore their impact on our hearts, we forfeit the forgiveness and healing we so desperately need. Even worse, we allow the Evil One to cripple us with his lies. He knows just what our dark secrets have led us to believe about ourselves. And he uses our daily circumstances to reinforce those lies. Satan is "the father of lies" (John 8:44), and he delights in paralyzing us with guilt and fear. Our biggest fear is that others will not only discover our secrets but will also find out who we really are.

The great news is that God delivered us from our sins the moment we trusted in Jesus Christ and confessed Him as Lord (Romans 10:9). Our sins have been forgiven *once and for all* by Jesus' sacrificial death on the cross (1 Peter 3:18). We have been reconciled to God because Jesus paid the penalty for us (Colossians 1:21–22)! Psalm 103:12 reminds us that "as far as the east is from the west, so far has he removed our transgressions from us." We can stand firmly and securely in this truth.

When we realize that God has freely forgiven us through Christ, we can truly forgive ourselves. I (Erin) was actually shocked to learn that the Bible never talks about forgiving ourselves. It speaks only of God's forgiveness and forgiving one another. If you're having a hard time forgiving yourself, it could be that you're rejecting Christ's forgiveness. It's like saying, "I know better than God whether I deserve to be forgiven!" What often gets in the way of receiving Christ's forgiveness is human pride. The remedy for pride is to humble ourselves before God and ask Him to forgive our sins.

First John 1:9 says that "if we confess our sins, [God] is faithful and just to forgive us our sins, and to purify us from all unrighteousness." When we confess our sins, past or present, to God, we can know for sure that He will hear and forgive us. We don't have to keep confessing our sins over and over. We must simply choose to trust God's promise. We might not *feel* forgiven, but God has declared it!

Don't be lulled into complacency, though. Satan will keep throwing your failures and sins in your face—or at least keep them rumbling around in the back of your mind. That's why he's also called "the accuser" (Revelation 12:10). But when he whispers his accusations in your ear, you have a choice: Will you believe Satan's lies or embrace God's forgiveness?

If you're struggling to forgive yourself, it may help to follow this two-step process:[6]

1. Identify the lies that have been written on your heart as a result of your choices and experiences. Then write them down to bring them out into the light.
2. Next, apply the truth of God to these lies. Find Scripture verses that speak truth to the lies and write them on index cards you can carry with you. Pull them out and review the verses whenever the lies begin to surface in your mind and heart.

In chapter 5 we discussed the devastating impact self-talk can have in our lives and marriages. These internal conversations we continually have with ourselves can be more vicious and unloving than anything our husbands might say. To combat negative self-talk, we need to fill our minds with God's truth. One powerful verse to counter the lies we believe about ourselves is Romans 8:1: "There is now no condemnation for those who are in Christ Jesus."[8]

Forgive Yourself . . . But Don't Forget These Verses

As far as the east is from the west, so far has he removed our transgressions from us. (Psalm 103:12)

In him we have redemption through his blood, the forgiveness of sins, in accordance with the riches of God's grace. (Ephesians 1:7)

Be kind and compassionate to one another, forgiving each other, just as in Christ God forgave you. (Ephesians 4:32)

If we confess our sins, he is faithful and just and will forgive us our sins and purify us from all unrighteousness. (1 John 1:9)

As we bring our darkest secrets out of the closet into the light of God's truth, we can find the grace to accept His forgiveness and even forgive ourselves. Letting go of self-condemnation frees us so that we can offer grace and forgiveness to our husbands.

Forgiving Your Spouse

Our husbands impact our lives in ways no one else can. I (Erin) can remember early in our marriage when Greg struggled with being completely honest with me over our finances. Unfortunately, what started as a small mistruth ended up having a major impact on our marriage. As we worked through this, I also began to learn a lot about forgiveness and grace on my part. Although I would not want to relive this experience, there were "treasures" that we both gained. As I learned through this, our husbands' behaviors and decisions can be life giving or heart crushing. Think about it—your husband has deeper access to your heart than almost any other human being. Whatever he says or does ultimately affects you. If he makes a poor financial decision, it affects you. If he lies, it affects you. If he has an affair, it affects you. However, there are also more minor offenses that may occur and they may still impact your heart—he may criticize you, be insensitive, use cutting or sarcastic words, or even at times in his preoccupation with work, not meet your needs. Although these are more minor, they still have the potential to hurt you. His decisions—for good or ill—have a great impact on you and your family.

As you and I know, being married inevitably involves risk. If we want to experience love and intimacy, we must also accept the risk of being hurt. Of course, this goes both ways. We, too, have the power to deeply wound our husbands' hearts. As we discussed earlier, the hurts inflicted in marriage often force us into a crisis of forgiveness. We can either erect walls to keep from being hurt again, or we can forgive. The choice is up to us.

Peter came to Jesus and asked, "Lord how many times shall I forgive my brother when he sins against me? Up to seven times?" Jesus answered, "I tell you, not seven times but seventy-seven times."

—Matthew 18:21–22

In a previous chapter we talked about the way anger creates a tangled web of knots inside us. When anger and bitterness take root in our hearts, we become exactly the opposite of who we desire to be. Harboring anger toward our husbands ultimately harms us more than it harms them. But forgiveness unties the knots and sets us free from the soul-damaging effects of anger. We must choose forgiveness not only because it's right but because it's for our own good.

Fuller Theological Seminary professor Lewis Smedes once said, "The first and often the only person to be healed by forgiveness is the person who does the forgiving. . . . When we genuinely forgive, we set a prisoner free and then discover that the prisoner we set free was us![7]

When your spouse hurts or offends you, we suggest following five basic steps to free yourself from anger, resentment, and an unforgiving spirit:[8]

Step 1: Analyze exactly what the offense was and define what you've actually lost. Identify how your husband hurt you. When you're harboring anger over an experience, it helps to identify what you feel was denied or taken from you. Ask yourself these questions:

- What was taken from me?
- What was I denied?
- Why am I feeling resentful?

Step 2: Allow yourself to grieve. Give yourself the chance to feel the hurt. Don't minimize or avoid the pain. Instead, try to describe your emotions. Journaling on paper or on the computer or writing a letter to your husband (which you don't actually give him) are some tools that can help you express your feelings.

When I (Erin) was working toward my master's degree in clinical psychology, the psychologist I was interning with encouraged me to engage in this process. She told me to write an anger letter. I wasn't to edit it, but just to let all of my feelings of anger pour out on the paper through my pen. I kept thinking this was a silly assignment, but later on in the week, something happened that caused me to write for more than two hours. I sealed that letter in an envelope and carried it with me to my next supervision visit with her.

My mentor asked me if I'd like to read my letter to her, and even though I knew there were details in the letter that weren't pretty, I began reading. Soon tears were flowing. Honestly, I cried throughout the rest of our meeting and for about the next twenty-four hours. Although my emotion wasn't entirely related to experiences in my marriage, it started there and led to other scenarios. That's how grief is—one circumstance or memory can trigger the tears, but as you allow yourself to spill your feelings, additional memories and sorrows come up as well. Grieving honestly and openly is like an internal cleansing of the soul. My mentor assured me that the tears would stop, and finally they did. I was exhausted when I was finished—but also greatly relieved.

Grieving is essential. Often we give ourselves permission to grieve when someone dies or moves away. However, my girlfriend and I will often say, "Life is one loss after another." Circumstances change, children grow up, dreams are lost, disappointment happens, and expectations are dashed. We must learn to grieve life's losses, changes, and hurts.

Step 3: Seek to understand your husband better. This step isn't an easy one. It will take some maturity to try to understand why your husband behaves the way he does. As you discover why he is the way he is, you can begin to experience empathy, and your own anger knots will gradually untie. This may even lead you to feel compassion toward your husband when he has hurt you. Was his offense similar to something that was done to him earlier in his life? Did he have a parent who also struggled with the same behavior? When he acted in a hurtful way, was he hungry, stressed, or getting sick? Understanding is not excusing. It's just understanding.

Step 4: Release your desire to get even or retaliate. The word *forgiveness* means to "untie," "loosen," or "release." When you refuse to forgive someone, that person is emotionally tied to you. Sometimes it's helpful to say aloud, "I forgive you!" We must choose to let go of our anger and our desire to get even with our husbands—even if they haven't apologized. This is more an act of the will than a feeling. If through this process you discover that you have something to apologize for (maybe a harsh tone in response or a critical statement or withdrawal of your affection), own it. Set the example for apologizing. Your husband may or may not follow suit. We encourage couples to use the following pattern to apologize: *I was wrong. I'm sorry. Please forgive me. I love you.* Be as specific as possible, naming your offense.

Step 5: Try to find the "pearls" in the offense. Finding something positive (or pearls) in our trials allows us heal even further. We cannot hold anger and gratefulness in our hearts at the same time—it's impossible. Maybe you gained a specific perspective by going through a painful situation or gained sensitivity toward others who are hurting in a way you were hurt. (We'll explore this concept we call "treasure-hunting" in depth in the next chapter).

Keep these steps handy because you *will* need them. Remember, for a marriage to thrive and remain healthy, forgiveness must be offered again and again.

Forgiveness in Your Marriage

Two imperfect people living under one roof in an intimate covenant relationship will create plenty of opportunities to practice forgiveness. For a successful marriage, forgiveness is more than just a necessity; it's a requirement. Think about any marriage that has ended up in divorce, and you'll likely find that a failure to offer or receive forgiveness played a major role.

Even in situations where one spouse has been unfaithful in the marriage, the response of the injured spouse can often determine whether reconciliation is possible. If forgiveness is offered and received, the marriage stands a good chance not only of being restored but of growing stronger. But both spouses must be willing to go through the painful process of forgiveness.

◇◇◇◇◇◇◇◇◇◇◇◇◇◇◇◇◇◇◇◇ ♥♥♥ ◇◇◇◇◇◇◇◇◇◇◇◇◇◇◇◇◇◇◇◇

A happy marriage is the union of two good forgivers.

—Ruth Bell Graham

◇◇◇◇◇◇◇◇◇◇◇◇◇◇◇◇◇◇◇◇ ♥♥♥ ◇◇◇◇◇◇◇◇◇◇◇◇◇◇◇◇◇◇◇◇

When Misty (whose story was shared earlier) confessed her two-year affair with her high-school sweetheart to her husband of ten years, she wondered how reconciliation could ever happen. It seemed impossible. But here's how their journey of forgiveness transpired:

Thinking back to that day still makes my stomach sick. It was a relief to be honest with my husband about what I was doing, but how would we ever put the pieces back together? I knew I wanted to fight for our marriage and our family. Thankfully Matt did, too. Neither of us wanted our two children to suffer the trauma of a divorce. Although Matt was hurt to the depths of his soul and very angry at me, he said he wanted to at least try to work through all of it with a counselor.

Although we were geographically in the Bible Belt, I felt as if I was in hell at times. News travels fast in a small town, and judgments can be harsh. People hurled accusations at me, and I felt as if I were wearing a scarlet letter whenever I walked into Walmart or my kids' schools. My dear husband dealt with some of the same harsh judgments, but from the other extreme: People looked at him strangely and wondered how he could ever forgive me.

Healing our marriage didn't happen overnight, but after six

years of hard work and pain, Matt and I have finally reconciled. I'm not proud of the choices I made, but I did make them. I don't think others understand that they, too, could end up on a journey like mine. Matt had to work through a lot of anger toward Tom and me, but he chose forgiveness. I had to seek forgiveness not only from Matt but from the Lord as well. And I also had to forgive Tom for participating in the affair and the people who judged me so harshly.

A godly counselor walked with Matt and me through this process, as well as many friends who set judgment aside and joined us in the fight for our marriage. The healing truly began to flood us after we attended a marriage intensive (*www.national marriage.com*). As Matt and I gained understanding into what was really going on in our marriage, it enabled us to take slow, steady steps forward. I will be the first to admit that I didn't believe forgiveness after an affair is possible. But it is!

Forgiveness in a marriage relationship is an absolute necessity, whether it's over major issues like infidelity or everyday issues like these:

- My husband forgot to shovel the driveway, so I had to do it.
- We had a fight because I overspent on groceries for the sixth month in a row.
- We planned a date night and my husband came home late.
- I was in a bad mood and snapped at my husband.
- We disagreed on how to respond to our fifteen-year-old daughter's disrespectful behavior.
- The baby was up three times last night, and my husband never moved.

Our willingness to forgive the small stuff in our marriages can significantly influence the quality of our relationships. In fact, the small offenses we encounter in marriage are often the ones that can build up over time and lead to resentment. If we can't forgive the minor offenses, how will we forgive the major ones?

We need to remind ourselves that we will hurt each other simply because we're imperfect. As Henry Cloud and John Townsend point out, "We can expect failure from even the best people in our lives."[9]

So how can we avoid an unforgiving spirit that leads to bitterness and a hardened heart? The best place to start is identifying the hurts we've caused in our marriages and seeking forgiveness. Ask the Lord to bring anything to your attention that you may not be aware of. Then reflect on the following questions to identify possible ways you've offended or hurt your husband.[10]

- Is there anything I haven't been doing in our marriage that I should be doing?
- Have I neglected any of my spouse's needs?
- Have I said critical or cruel things to my spouse?
- Have I withheld anything from my spouse? Encouragement? Affirmation? Physical affection? Love?
- Am I currently doing anything that has a negative impact on my marriage?

As you identify words or actions that may have caused harm, whether intentionally or unintentionally, seek your husband's forgiveness. Also ask if you've hurt or offended him in any other ways. Keep an open heart and mind toward your husband, and be prepared for honesty. Set aside the urge to explain or defend your actions. Simply listen and receive what he has to say, and try to draw out how he felt as a result of your behavior. Own what you can take responsibility for, and apologize for hurts you've caused.

God is passionate about reconciliation. He wants us to seek forgiveness and make amends for our hurtful actions and words. In fact, it's more important to Him than religious activity. In the Sermon on the Mount, Jesus said,

If you are offering your gift at the altar and there remember
that your brother has something against you, leave your gift
there in front of the altar. First go and be reconciled to your
brother; then come and offer your gift. (Matthew 5:23–24)

God also wants us to acknowledge our own hurt feelings and
choose to forgive our husbands. There are times when we can and
should overlook an offense, especially if it's minor (Proverbs 19:11).
At other times, we may be able to forgive minor offenses without
confronting husbands, especially if we know they were unintentional.
Colossians 3:13 tells us to "bear with each other and forgive whatever
grievances you may have against one another." One way to forgive
minor grievances is to articulate our feelings through journaling or
prayer. This is similar to grieving a loss.

*Marriage is three parts love and
seven parts forgiveness.*

—Langdon Mitchell

Be aware that your husband may not have intentionally hurt you
and may have no idea that he did. Many times we're blind to the
offenses we cause others. If your relationship is in a healthy place, you
may want to gently share a minor frustration or hurt with him. If you
do, make sure to use "I" statements—"I was hurt when you didn't
notice or thank me for cleaning the entire house."

Don't just launch into a confrontation or, as Greg likes to say, "draft
your husband into a battle he didn't know was there." Simply let him
know you've been working through a forgiveness exercise, and you're
wondering if you might share with him a few things you realize have

hurt you. If he isn't willing to hear your feelings or apologize, don't let that stop you from forgiving him. Remember: Forgiveness is a choice.

When offenses cause deep hurt, we clearly need to bring the issue to our husbands' attention. If we don't address an issue, it may lead to bitterness and resentment. Lack of forgiveness can also cause us to close off our hearts toward our husbands.

In Matthew 18:15, Jesus said, "If your brother sins against you, go and show him his fault, just between the two of you. If he listens to you, you have won your brother over." When you approach your husband, clearly state that your purpose in bringing the issue to his attention is to resolve anger and bitterness so you can have a more loving and intimate relationship. Again, he may or may not be willing to apologize or seek forgiveness, but you have the opportunity to give the gift of forgiveness anyway. If he does ask for forgiveness, celebrate this by sharing a special dinner together or an evening of intimacy!

Remember: Forgiveness is a journey that continues throughout marriage. It can also be a healing salve for even the most minor offenses. So keep short accounts in your relationship and forgive on a regular basis so that your hearts will remain open toward each other. Don't allow a spirit of unforgiveness to grow roots of bitterness and resentment in your marriage. Let forgiveness set you free to enjoy a more loving relationship!

◇◇◇◇◇◇◇◇◇◇◇◇◇◇◇◇◇◇◇◇ ♥ ♥ ♥ ◇◇◇◇◇◇◇◇◇◇◇◇◇◇◇◇◇◇◇◇

Treasure Hunting

Let's face it: life is difficult. It knocks us down and sucks the energy out of us. It distorts our perspectives and damages our sense of worth. We can become so focused on the trials we encounter in our marriages and the conflict they can create that it can be difficult to recognize the blessings when they come.

But *every* difficulty we experience in life has the potential to be transformed into something beautiful—to create a pearl. Pearls are formed by a very slow natural process that begins when an irritating grain of sand gets inside an oyster. In response, the oyster secretes layer after layer of calcium carbonate to coat the sand until, after two or three years, a pearl is born!

Life can certainly irritate us like a grain of sand in an oyster, but creating pearls out of pain isn't necessarily a natural process for humans. Yet as we allow God to work in our lives and marriages, He transforms trials into blessings. This is a promise that God makes in James 1:12, "Blessed is the man who perseveres under trial, for when he has stood the test he will receive the crown of life, that God has promised to those who love him." God *will* do His part—He will bless us in some way; our part is to do what we like to call "treasure hunting." The treasures we discover not only benefit us individually, but they can also lead to greater love and intimacy in our marriages.

Treasure-Hunting Your Trials

I (Erin) have a good friend, Laura, who found such a treasure within weeks of a heart-wrenching loss. But that positive perspective came only after surviving many other painful blows in her life. Laura's first husband had been involved in numerous affairs, and even though Laura fought to keep her marriage together, he ended up leaving her and their young daughter. Laura was devastated but turned to God for help. She knew it wasn't going to be easy, but she trusted that God would never leave or forsake her.

In this world you will have trouble.

—John 16:33

After the divorce, Laura was forced to sell her dream home overlooking a lake and also had to find a job to support herself and her daughter. She accepted a position as a professor of psychology at a local university, and life finally seemed as if it was returning to normal. She was content trusting God to meet her needs.

Eventually she met an engineering professor at the university who was deeply loved and respected by students and faculty. He had been through a brutal divorce, but Laura knew immediately that this was a man she could give her heart to. They began dating and soon were engaged. Their wedding day was a fabulous celebration of God's redemptive love and new beginnings for both of them. Laura was most struck by Paul's deep love for Jesus. That passion flowed into their marriage relationship, and Laura felt loved in a way she had never been loved before.

During the early years of their marriage, they lost their home in a tornado and then purchased lake-front property that became Laura's dream home. They also continued working at the university. Life had never been better.

One day after about four years of marriage, Paul and Laura drove together to the university as they did most days. Before heading to their departments, they kissed and said good-bye. Little did they know this would be their final good-bye.

During one of Laura's classes, a frantic coworker motioned Laura out into the hallway and informed her that Paul had collapsed from an apparent heart attack. Laura rushed to his side and prayed over him while paramedics attempted to save his life on the way to the hospital. Despite their heroic efforts, Paul died. Laura's precious husband was gone.

About a week later, Laura sent me this email:

> Although I am heartbroken and in complete shock, I can see
> that these have been the best four years of my life. Round after
> round of CPR brought no hope, but I was able to pray my
> sweet husband into heaven, and I have to believe that he could
> hear me. He loved Jesus so much, and that allowed him to love
> me in a way I had never experienced love. The night before
> Paul died, I wondered if life could get any better. I was living a
> dream, and it was all because of Jesus in our lives. He allowed
> us to love one another with an everlasting love.

Can you see the pearls Laura found amid the painful trials in her life? Divorce was devastating, but she developed a deeper relationship with God and learned to stand on her own two feet. She had to sell her dream home but learned that happiness isn't ultimately in "stuff." Her teaching position at the university was what eventually brought Paul into her life. She and Paul lost their home to a tornado, but their new property on the lake was like the home she'd been forced to sell after the divorce.

Losing Paul so unexpectedly has been a huge blow, but Laura is deeply grateful for four wonderful years with him and experiencing such a special love. Laura has experienced God's faithfulness in her life and knows that Jesus will walk with her into the future.

The trials you've experienced may differ from Laura's. But as Laura discovered, you can transform them into blessings as you search for the treasure that's hidden deep within them. God is able to use every experience in your life, no matter how hard or painful, to draw you closer to Him and show you how precious you are to Him. When you realize how much He loves and treasures you, you'll find His love flowing through you to your husband and others in your life.

C. S. Lewis has been famously quoted as saying, "God whispers to us in our pleasures, speaks in our conscience, but shouts in our pains."[1] When we're in pain, we're desperate for truthful answers to the hard questions in life. We need to know whether God is really there, and that He is good.

Facing trials is one important way we learn that God is truly able to redeem our pain, giving us "a crown of beauty instead of ashes, . . . and a garment of praise instead of a spirit of despair" (Isaiah 61:3). As we experience God's loving faithfulness in the midst of our pain, we understand the reality of His promise "that in all things God works for the good of those who love him" (Romans 8:28).

Treasure hunting is another way we experience the reality of God's love for us. As we unearth the pearls that have formed in our lives through painful trials, we discover the countless ways God is working all of our trials together for good.

The principle of treasure hunting is quite simple, but it does require a willingness to see our trials from God's perspective, as well as an investment of our effort. As I (Gary) wrote in my book *Your Relationship with God*,

> Treasure hunting with God involves an investment of my heart and will. I must choose to trust him, even when I can't see what he's doing—which is often the case. When I accept the fact that God is sovereign and he knows what is best for me, I then begin to discover the treasure he has cultivated in me like a precious pearl.[4]

Are you ready to treasure-hunt your trials? Following are some steps to finding the hidden pearls in your life.[5] First write down the painful or difficult trials you have experienced in the past or are going through right now. Things like . . .

- Sexual or physical assault or abuse
- Financial difficulties or bankruptcy
- Job loss or getting fired
- Being bullied
- Death of a child, family member or loved one
- Personal illness, disability or mental health issue
- Prodigal son or daughter
- Infidelity
- Drug or alcohol addiction
- Divorce

It can be overwhelming to list all of your trials, so you may want to start off by focusing on one or two. The trials you write about may be experiences that caused great anger, hurt, shame, fear, or feelings of worthlessness, or they could be things you deeply dislike about yourself or your spouse. Some trials may feel too painful to list right now, so start with one that doesn't stir up excessive grief, anger, or despair. Take an honest look at this trial, and write down all the facts you can recall. What happened specifically, and how did it affect you emotionally? Avoid exaggerating the facts or letting your emotions lead you into a downward spiral of negative thoughts, such as *This is the worst thing that ever happened to me, My life is over,* or *This is hopeless. Nothing will ever get better.* This tendency toward negative and hopeless thinking is often what prompts counselors to caution couples against using words like "always" or "never" when describing marital problems. Be honest about your trials, but don't allow your thoughts to run wild. Just state the facts as accurately and fairly as possible.

Trials started early in my (Gary's) life. I grew up in a home where education wasn't valued. Neither of my parents went very far in school, so I wasn't encouraged to excel academically. I didn't have a lot of support to do well—and I didn't. On top of that, my family moved frequently. I changed schools almost every year—sometimes two or three times a year. This constant transition hit me hardest around the third grade. We lived in California during a time when education focused on boosting self-esteem rather than measuring academic performance.

After a year in that system, my family moved to Washington state, where a much more rigorous educational climate existed. I performed poorly in my initial assessment at school and had to repeat third grade. I felt stupid and embarrassed. I had actually flunked third grade! Even my grown children teased me about flunking the third grade when they found out. But treasure hunting enabled me to discover the benefits that came out of this painful event in my life. Most important, it set me free from the shame and humiliation that lay buried in my heart for so many years.

As you think about the trials that have caused you difficulty and pain, it's also important to avoid the blame game. Don't beat yourself up over past mistakes or waste time blaming your parents or husband for what happened. Blaming will sabotage your treasure hunt and will lead to bitterness and resentment. Our trials can only be transformed into blessings only as we let go of blame and bitterness through forgiveness and focus instead on finding the treasure God has hidden within the trials.

As you describe the trial, be prepared to experience a range of emotions. Identify each emotion as it emerges—we call this "naming your pain"—and allow yourself to really feel it. Don't deny the pain or hurry through it. Healing can't be rushed; it's a process you need to walk through one step at a time. You may be able to work through a minor trial in fifteen minutes, but it may take months or even years for a deep wound to heal. It's important to take as much time as you need to find the treasure in your trial.

Allow yourself to grieve. Express your anger and hurt or any other emotion you feel. Let your tears flow freely. You may find it helpful to express your feelings verbally or in writing. Pouring out your feelings to God in prayer is also a healthy way to work through grief and hurt. Even though the Lord knows all about your experiences, He wants you to talk to Him and tell Him everything you're thinking and feeling.
To begin, think about some good things that have come out of your trials. If you can't see any at first, think about character qualities that have been developed or refined in your life through each fiery trial. Has God grown the fruit of His Spirit in your life through your trials— "love, joy, peace, patience, kindness, goodness, faithfulness, gentleness and self-control" (Galatians 5:22–23)?

Perhaps you've gained wisdom, greater compassion and understanding for others, or a deeper love and respect for your husband. Or you may realize that the trials you've endured have drawn you closer to the Lord and taught you to trust Him more in every area of your life. Maybe a particular trial brought you and your husband closer together or taught you greater empathy and patience. Perhaps you've always struggled with pride, thinking you had it all together and always knew what to do in every situation, but a trial humbled you and taught you that God is the only one with all the answers. Through that trial, you may have learned how to depend on Him moment by moment rather than relying entirely on yourself.

You might discover that a trial has made you . . .

- More empathetic—increased awareness of others' needs and pain
- More courageous
- More patient
- More humble—God gives His grace to the humble (James 4:6)
- Stronger and more durable as a person
- Less likely to make hurtful comments or to criticize
- More certain of God's presence
- Slower to speak and quicker to listen
- More responsible and mature
- More loving

The benefits are endless! The treasure is often right there in front of you if you'll just look.

If a trial has caused extensive damage in your life, you may find it especially difficult to find anything good that's come from it. This was the case for Linda. When I (Gary) met Linda, she was a college student struggling with discouragement and depression.[4] The burden she was carrying was so heavy that she didn't have the strength to keep going. She knew she needed help, but she had never divulged the secret that was eating away at her: Her father, an alcoholic with a sexual addiction, had molested her over a period of years. She felt ashamed, angry, and ruined by the horrible behavior of someone who should have cared for her and protected her.

Linda wondered how to move forward with her life and not let the past destroy her future. By coming to me, Linda was beginning to assume responsibility for how she had responded to what happened to her. She didn't know how to handle the painful memories or the negative emotions they caused. She felt so damaged that marriage seemed impossible. "I feel so unworthy," Linda told me. "I feel that if I meet the right guy, someone I really like, as soon as he finds out what happened to me, he'll think I'm trash."[5]

Linda and I began meeting regularly. Ultimately, since God promises that He will turn every negative experience we encounter into something good, I wanted her to discover the "treasure" from this devastating experience in order to deal with her shame and anger and move toward forgiveness. But let me be clear about something. This didn't mean Linda's father's abuse was okay or should be excused in any way. And it didn't mean diminishing the wrong or denying the pain she felt. But treasure hunting allowed Linda to see that just as God brought good out of evil in Joseph's life (Genesis 37–50), He could bring something beautiful out of the evil that happened in her life. Only God can bring beauty out of ashes. I'll never forget some of the treasures that emerged for Linda. Over the course of several meetings, she began to realize that as a result of the abuse, she possessed a very close relationship with the Lord. "The Lord is near to the brokenhearted" (Psalm 34:18). She possessed a strength and confidence that she is able to survive difficult circumstances, "because with God all things are possible" (Matthew 19:26). She also saw that she has a greater compassion and understanding for others who have been molested or abused. These were just some of the many "pearls" that Linda embraced as the result of God's love and provision. "He gives strength to the weary and increases the power of the weak" (Isaiah 40:29).

Take a thorough look at yourself as Linda did and list every positive and valuable quality you can think of. If you find yourself struggling to list more than a few good qualities, ask for input from people who know you well, such as your spouse, close friends, your parents, a godly mentor, or a counselor. They can often find treasure you might never see because they have the advantage of objective distance. As the old adage goes, you may not be able to see the forest for the trees. When you're lost in a wilderness of painful memories, it can be impossible to find your way without help.

We cannot control what happens to us, but we can choose to find treasure in the painful trials in our lives.

Trials come in all shapes and sizes. Some cause ongoing frustration; others plunge us into despair. You may feel as if your problems are minor compared to others, but if they consume your thoughts, cause irritation or pain, or affect the way you relate to your husband, you need to address them rather than ignore them. Walking through trials—no matter what the size—is how we grow.

This is the heart and soul of treasure hunting. But looking for the benefits can be difficult, especially if you've experienced traumatic events in your life. Pain, depression, and negative thinking can blind you to the ways God is transforming these events into something good in your life. Even if you haven't been through terribly painful trials, it can still be challenging to find treasure in hurtful experiences. But, Romans 12:3 (NLT) offers this wise advice: "Be honest in your evaluation of yourselves, measuring yourselves by the faith God has given [you]."

The benefits we discover from our trials aren't intended to bless us alone; they're meant to bless others as well. God has a special way of using the trials in our lives to teach us to love and serve others. He also knows how to use the treasures we've discovered to help others hunt for the treasures in their own trials.

Trials to Treasures
Gary Smalley

How can our trials benefit others? This can happen in a number of ways. Take my example of being a poor student. I was a horrible reader and speller all the way through high school and into junior college. After a year and a half in junior college, my grade-point average was only 1.6. I didn't know how to study, so a kindergarten teacher tutored me. The next semester I achieved a 2.4, and things went up from there.

So how could my poor academic beginning help others? The treasure-hunting process made me realize that because reading and writing were so hard for me growing up, I know how important it is to write books that people can understand and relate to. This might not be the case if I were a real academic type.

When I started writing books about relationships, I worked hard to make the principles easy to understand and to tell interesting stories so the truths would come to life. Since I wasn't good at grammar, I always enlisted the help of a team of writers who had that expertise. But I was never satisfied with a chapter until it communicated simply and in an interesting way. And you know what? My books sold— even into the millions!

Remember Linda, who suffered childhood sexual abuse? Her journey toward healing was long and difficult, but over time she came to find the pearls in her pain. Now she's extremely compassionate and sensitive to the pain of others. In fact, she can intuitively sense when she crosses paths with a woman who bears the hidden wounds of abuse. She truly understands what abused women are going through because she's been there. Her deep desire to help others led her to volunteer at a woman's crisis center, where she offers hope to those whose lives have been shattered by various kinds of abuse. Linda's trials and the treasure she has discovered are bringing hope and healing to others.

This is what the apostle Paul was talking about when he wrote that God "comforts us in all our troubles, so that we can comfort those in any trouble with the comfort which we ourselves have received from God" (2 Corinthians 1:4).

Now that you know how to hunt for buried treasure in your life, keep hunting! The more you hunt, the more treasure you'll find. Treasure hunting is a lifelong adventure, not just a one-time exercise. So don't settle for just one lovely pearl. Let God transform all your trials into blessings!

Helping Your Husband Treasure-Hunt

Ecclesiastes reminds us that "two are better than one, because they have a good return for their work: If one falls down, his friend can help him up" (4:9–10). When it comes to treasure hunting in marriage, two are definitely better than one! Chances are, your husband has experienced his share of painful trials in life, and even if you can't fully understand the damage they've done, you can help him walk through them toward healing.

Just as you've learned that God can transform your trials into blessings, you can encourage your husband to treasure-hunt his own trials to find the good God wants to bring out of them. How your husband has responded to trials is his responsibility. You can't fix his past or erase his pain and make everything better for him. It may be tempting to do his treasure hunting for him and point out the benefits he may be oblivious to. But ultimately, it's up to him to find the pearls in his pain. Your role is simply to offer your support and encouragement as your husband learns to treasure-hunt his own trials.

Do you remember the crisis in George Bailey's life in the movie *It's a Wonderful Life?*[6] The corrupt banker Mr. Potter hatches a scheme to take over the Bailey family savings-and-loan business. When George's careless uncle Billy loses the mortgage payment, George realizes that financial ruin and prison are inevitable. He comes home from work on the edge of despair. He snaps at his wife, Mary, yells at his daughter who is practicing the piano, and rages at the loose stairway post. The post had been loose for years, but this time when he inadvertently yanks it off, his anger boils over. Mary is confused and upset over George's uncharacteristic behavior. But she has no idea what her husband is dealing with. She doesn't know that for all practical purposes, their future and that of the entire town is about to disintegrate. George feels as if he is carrying the weight of the world on his shoulders, and he's driven to the brink of suicide.

When Mary realizes that something is seriously wrong with George, she starts making phone calls and asking questions. In the end, she discovers the reason for George's outrageous behavior and enlists help from the townspeople to save the business. The very people George has helped through their own trials and hardships rescue him in a time of great need. But without Mary, George's life would have been destroyed. In his darkest moment, his wife was his biggest help.

George Bailey's situation may seem extreme, but it illustrates the important role we can play in our husbands' lives. Proverbs 20:5 says, "The purposes of a man's heart are deep waters, but a man [or woman] of understanding draws them out." As a wholehearted wife, you can be your husband's biggest support and encouragement in the trials of life. And one of the best ways to encourage him is to help him treasure-hunt!

Although the steps will be the same for both of you, keep in mind that how your husband treasure-hunts his trials may differ significantly from the way you do it. Differences in gender and personality will also factor into the way each of you treasure-hunts. Regardless of how he chooses to work through the steps, allow him the freedom to do it in a way that feels best to him.

Here are some ways you can help your husband treasure-hunt his trials:

1. *Learn more about your husband's background.* One of the greatest aspects of love is being known and understood. Seek to know your husband more deeply and understand the impact his experiences have had on him. Draw him out regarding painful or difficult trials and traumas from his past, including experiences growing up. Encourage him to describe what happened and how the experience made him feel. Also ask him what impact each trial has had on his life. Keep in mind that some experiences—such as physical or sexual abuse, being bullied, or the death of someone close to him—may be too painful or shame-filled for him to talk about. War experiences, in particular, can be extremely traumatic and may trigger painful flashbacks. If your husband has experienced major traumas in his life, he might benefit from counseling or a support group. However, many men view counseling as a sign of weakness, so tread carefully if you suggest it. If you frame it as something that will help him get past the painful memories and move on with his life, he might be more willing to consider it.

2. *Ask about difficulties your husband may be going through right now.* Be sensitive to current issues that may be bothering him. Ask insightful questions about what is happening and how he feels about it. What is making him feeling discouraged? Are there circumstances

in his life right now that are triggering negative or unhealthy reactions? Is he unusually preoccupied or short-tempered? Has he become more withdrawn and disengaged from life? Do your best to find out why. Right in the middle of his emotional funk is probably not the best time to pester him with questions, however. Pray for God's timing and wisdom and look for an appropriate moment when you can ask him what is prompting him to behave or feel a certain way. If your husband focuses on blaming others for his problems, gently nudge him to look beyond what's been done and consider a productive way forward. For example, if he's upset about a decision his boss made, acknowledge his frustration, but then say, "I guess you can't change what happened, but we could pray and brainstorm about how God would have us respond." Rather than criticizing him for reacting negatively to a trial, try to understand and acknowledge his feelings, express your love and support, and honestly affirm his value.

3. *Allow for differences in the way your husband processes his emotions regarding a painful experience.* As a man, he'll likely express his emotions differently, so don't expect him to grieve or feel other emotions the same way you do. His emotions may be just as intense as yours, but he may process them more subtly over a period of time. He may shed tears as well, but perhaps not quite as freely as you do, especially if this is out of his comfort zone. Allow him to own his feelings about his trials. Don't tell him how you think he should feel or process his experiences. If he's struggling to identify his feelings, offer suggestions without forcing your own perceptions on him.

4. *Help your husband avoid extremes.* Help your husband recount the facts of an experience as accurately as possible without exaggerating what happened. If he's angry, encourage him to express it in healthy ways. Then calmly restate the facts as you heard them and clarify his feelings as objectively as possible. Instead of saying, "Yes, your dad always did play favorites," you might say, "So, it sounds as if what's

really bugging you about your father is that he seems to have a pattern of favoring your brother." Or instead of saying in a panic, "We're going to lose the house if you don't do something!" you could calmly observe, "So if things continue to be as tight as they are right now, we need to be ready to put the house on the market. But we might know more in three months, right?" You can encourage your husband to avoid extremes by keeping a spiritual perspective in the midst of trials. That doesn't mean mouthing empty spiritual platitudes. It simply means that no matter how bad things are, you can choose to trust the Lord to walk with you and your husband through every trial. Remember that no matter how bad things get, you haven't lost everything. In the end, even the worst tragedies in life can never take away what God has given us in Christ!

5. *Let your husband work through his trials in his own time and way.* Don't force him to talk about his experiences or treasure-hunt the benefits and blessings in them if he's clearly not ready. Focus on encouraging him and honoring him in tangible ways without pressuring him to treasure-hunt. On the other hand, don't gloss over his trials.

6. *Discuss the possible benefits and blessings your husband might find in his trials.* Ask how he feels he's grown as a result of a painful experience. What character qualities have developed through his trials? How has his relationship with God changed? If he's open to your input, share some of the benefits you've discovered from your own trials and offer observations about some of the possible benefits you see coming from his trials. If you and your husband are spiritually unified as a couple, offer a spiritual perspective as well, discussing the ways God may be working a particular trial for good in your husband's life.

7. *Affirm your husband's strengths and positive qualities.* As wives we can tend to focus on our husbands' negative traits, criticizing their flaws rather than affirming their strengths. Fight that tendency. Instead, let your husband know what you appreciate about him. Does he have a

great sense of humor? Does he work hard to provide for your family? Has he been faithful and steady through hard times? Tell him. Note the strengths and character qualities you see in him. Ask what he values about the way God made him. Suggest that he ask others for their insights and observations about his strengths as well. Encourage him to make a list of trusted friends he could ask for support, in addition to you, as he treasure-hunts his trials.

8. *Encourage him to use what he has learned from his trials to help others.* Affirm the ways he already gives of himself or is reaching out to others in response to an adversity in his own life. Maybe he shows kindness to others in unique ways because he experienced unkindness as a child. Or perhaps he helps kids who are struggling academically because he struggled in school as well. He may not be aware that a painful trial in his life has ignited a passion to help others who are going through similar experiences. Help him connect the dots so he can see the benefits and blessings that have come from his trials.

9. *Pray for your husband, asking the Lord to guide his treasure hunting.* Ask God to open his heart and eyes to see how He is working in your husband's life. Pray that your husband will be able to see in tangible ways that God truly is able to bring good from any trial, no matter how painful.

As you and your husband discover the pearls that life's adversities have formed in your lives individually, you'll also begin to see how God is transforming the trials in your marriage into blessings. As we wrap up this treasure-hunting discussion, let's explore how you can hunt for treasure in your marriage by embracing the trials you experience as a couple.

Embracing Trials Together

Trials are among the most powerful tools God uses to shape and refine us into the image of Christ. This is as true in marriage as it is for us as individuals. If we want to know Jesus more intimately, we must be willing to embrace suffering and pain in this life just as He did when He came to Earth. In fact, as we follow in Christ's footsteps, we should expect trials.

The apostle Peter spoke extensively on the topic of suffering in his epistles. In one place he said, "Dear friends, do not be surprised at the painful trial you are suffering, as though something strange were happening to you. But rejoice that you participate in the sufferings of Christ" (1 Peter 4:12–13). Trials are not only an inevitable part of our lives because we live in a fallen world, but they're also woven into the fabric of our lives as followers of Christ.

Consider what John Piper wrote in his book *Desiring God*,

> I've never heard anyone say, "The really deep lessons of life have come through times of ease and comfort." But I have heard strong saints say, "Every significant advance I have ever made in [grasping] the depth of God's love and growing deep with Him has come through suffering."[7]

Most of us can see this is true from our own experience. Trials can indeed draw us closer to the Lord and to each other as a couple. But they also have the capacity to break our marriages apart. What enables us to withstand the destructive forces of our trials? What is the key to avoiding negative outcomes and instead experiencing deeper intimacy with God and our spouses as a result of our trials? How can we embrace the hardships of life—the inevitable pressure points, losses, disappointments, wounds, and pain—and become more Christlike because of them?

To find treasure in the trials we face in marriage, we need to hunt for the hidden blessings in them as a couple, just as we've learned to treasure-hunt individually. The good news is that we can make these choices even in the midst of our pain. The following steps can help you as a couple embrace your trials and begin to find the pearls in them. We realize that some of these principles may be difficult to implement when a husband and wife don't share the same faith. If that describes your marriage, don't be discouraged. Use these principles as prayer points for your marriage, and seek to apply them in your own life even if your husband isn't a believer.

1. Build a firm foundation in the Lord. In Matthew 7:24–25, Jesus said, "Everyone who hears these words of mine and puts them into practice is like a wise man who built his house on the rock. The rain came down, the streams rose, and the winds blew and beat against that house; yet it did not fall, because it had its foundation on the rock."

When we make a habit of listening to Jesus and obeying Him, we're laying a solid foundation in our marriages that will help us weather life's inevitable storms. FamilyLife founder Dennis Rainey notes that a solid spiritual foundation helped his wife, Barbara, and him face devastating news about their fifteen-year-old son. Samuel had always been a good athlete, so when Dennis and Barbara began noticing some problems, they decided to take him to a neurologist. Dennis writes,

> Suddenly, words we only heard once a year during the Jerry Lewis Telethon were echoing loudly. Samuel had muscular dystrophy. Barbara and I knew that our marriage was strong even before this particular storm hit us. From the beginning of our marriage, we have resolved to build our lives and our family upon God's Word and upon daily prayer together. When I hear of couples who buckle under the storms of life, my suspicion is they have not put down a firm foundation for their home.[8]

Build a firm spiritual foundation in your marriage before trials come your way. Wholeheartedly pursue God and His truth in all kinds of weather, not just when storms hit.

2. Cling to God. Hardship has a way of making us feel desperate and needy. When you and your husband are facing desperate times in your marriage, seek God together and cling to Him. Even if you haven't laid a firm spiritual foundation, it's *never* too late to turn to Him. God is rich in mercy and compassion (Exodus 34:6). In fact, trials are one of the ways God, in His mercy, pushes us toward Him.

"Let's pray" is one of the best phrases we (Greg and Erin) have used in the midst of our own worries and burdens in our marriage. Philippians 4:6 (NLT) reminds us, "Don't worry about anything; instead, pray about everything. Tell God what you need, and thank him for all he has done." If your husband won't pray with you, ask if you can pray on behalf of both of you. Cry out for God's help, direction, wisdom, strength, and comfort. And comfort each other with His Word.

3. Choose to move toward each other. Just as we have different personalities and bents, we have different ways of coping with stress, grief, and suffering. Allow for those differences. Respect the fact that your husband may cope very differently from you. What relieves stress or helps you process grief may not do the same for your husband. But don't allow yourself to isolate. Reach out to your husband and try to understand his feelings and needs. Choose to express love in a way he can receive. Take steps toward each other in the midst of your trials, even if you respond to them differently.

Dennis Rainey made a deliberate choice to move toward his wife and talk with her about their son's disease even though he didn't feel ready to talk.[9] Dennis's actions reflected sacrificial love, which can be difficult for spouses to demonstrate when they're struggling with their own pain and grief. If your husband isn't ready to talk about a situation, you may need to give him grace and do your processing with a trusted friend instead of weighing him down with it all.

4. Realize that you and your husband are in your trials together. As we mentioned earlier in the book, you and your husband are on the same team in your marriage. God created this unique relationship so that we wouldn't have to walk through life—or our trials—alone. No matter what you're going through together or individually, you share each other's burdens. Both of you share the pain of financial loss, illness, grief, in-law problems, or any number of other trials. Shared pain often becomes a bond that draws us closer together as husbands and wives. One couple who lost a child said that what kept them together through this horribly painful time was realizing that their spouse was the only other person who knew their son as well as they did and could understand the immense loss.

5. *Turn to your friends for support.* Some friends may reach out to you during a painful time in your marriage—especially when the crisis is obvious, such as death or illness. But if a struggle is more subtle or hidden, you and your spouse may need to initiate reaching out to others for help, comfort, prayer, encouragement, wisdom, or even a break from being consumed by the pain. Don't suffer in silence or isolate yourselves in a time of need. Being open to receiving comfort from others is a sign of humility and maturity. It blesses you and bonds you together with others. Galatians 6:2 reminds us to "carry each other's burdens, and in this way you will fulfill the law of Christ."

Our (Greg and Erin's) friends, who were experiencing a stressful life transition, attended a lip-sync show that their church youth group put on as a missions-trip fundraiser. That group of kids will probably never know how much their humorous renditions helped a stressed-out couple laugh together and experience relief from the anxiety and pressure of their circumstances. The church ministers in all kinds of ways.

6. *Trust God's sovereignty even in the mysteries of life.* We can't explain why God allows suffering or particular trials, but we can reaffirm our trust in Him even when we don't understand what's happening. We can remind ourselves that God is and always has been sovereign. Some ways you and your husband can do this are by reading the Bible and

praying together, attending church, listening to Bible teaching on the radio or the Internet, or reading other Christ-centered books on suffering together. When we can't see the big picture, God does. When we can't figure out what He's doing or what good can come out of our circumstances, we can see evidence of His goodness in other ways— biblically, historically, and in the world around us. Cling to the truth of God's sovereignty both individually and as a couple.

7. *Keep interacting with God.* God can handle our anger and every question that has ever been thrown at Him. Don't turn away in resentful silence. Turn to Him together and pour out your hearts. If it helps you or your spouse, use the psalms as your prayer book. They are full of raw, unfiltered emotion. It may seem easier for you or your spouse to talk to others about why you're mad at God than to talk to Him directly. But wrestling with Him directly keeps you in relationship. If you talk only to others about your issues with God, it's like trying to solve your marriage problems without ever talking to your spouse. Some wrestling with God will be done alone or with your spouse. But when you're ready, you may want to share with others how God is ministering to you in your trial.

8. *Choose to see the good in the midst of pain.* When tragedy strikes, many comment on how overwhelmed they are by the love of other people. God often ministers to us through others. This is one "good" that can come from trials. And so is God's unique ability to comfort us directly. As Mary Beth Chapman wrote in *Choosing to See*, nothing made the tragic death of their beloved daughter Maria feel "worth it," but Mary Beth could still acknowledge that good had come out of it. Relationships were forged in grief, their family received comfort, life took on a new perspective, and many people were ministered to through their pain.[10] Seeing the good in our trials doesn't erase loss or diminish pain, but it can be its own separate blessing. Thank God— together if at all possible—for the blessings in the midst of pain.

9. Reminisce. As time passes and the rawness of pain eases, take some time to look back together on your married life and the circumstances—joyous and difficult—that God has brought you through. Stop to consider the mysterious route that life has likely taken and how God has been faithful and present in it all—even when you couldn't see the end of the road. Reaffirm your trust in Him. Praise Him for His goodness. This could be a terrific date-night theme or anniversary celebration: looking back and praising God.

Part of the legacy you leave for others to see is how God led you through life's trials. Look at the testimony of Corrie ten Boom—a godly woman who experienced the horrors of the Holocaust.[11] God didn't allow Corrie to escape that pain, but He did walk with her through it, answering many prayers and using her to reach others during and after those trying years. Looking back can help you and your husband see God's faithfulness more clearly.

*Precious memories may remain even
of a bad home, if only the heart knows
how to find what is precious.*

—Fyodor Dostoyevsky, *The Brothers Karamazov*

10. Set your hope on the eternal. In Paul's first letter to Timothy, he counseled Timothy to "command those who are rich in this present world not to . . . put their hope in wealth, which is so uncertain, but to put their hope in God" (6:17). Not only are riches uncertain, but most aspects of our lives in this world are. We really don't know what the immediate future holds or how quickly life could change. This doesn't need to be a reason for anxiety, because we do know who holds the future, and we have the promise that He will never leave us or forsake us (Hebrews 13:5). Jesus tells us to "store up for yourselves treasures in heaven, where moth and rust do not destroy, and where thieves do not break in and steal. For where your treasure is, there your heart will be also" (Matthew 6:20–21). As believers who love the Lord and remain steadfast in trusting Him, we have a sure and certain hope that Christ has secured for us (Hebrews 6:19; Titus 2:11–14). Remind yourselves daily of that future hope!

Trials have a silver lining when you begin to see them through God's eyes. Invite Him to take every painful trial in your life—past, present, and future—and transform them into glittering pearls. Nothing is impossible for Him!

As you and your spouse treasure-hunt together, discovering the many blessings hidden within each trial, you'll not only come to know God and each other in a deeper way, but you'll also become channels for His love and grace.

Your treasure-hunting journey has just begun!

A More Loving Relationship Begins with You

I (Erin) am so honored to have shared this journey with you. This book has turned out to be so much richer and more satisfying than I ever dreamed it would be. The hours that have been poured into this project are enormous, but the Lord has brought about amazing blessings from it—even in my own marriage. I love how He does not waste anything to train us and teach us and continue to grow us! Ephesians 4:14-16 in *The Message* says,

> No prolonged infancies among us, please. We'll not tolerate babes in the woods, small children who are an easy mark for impostors. God wants us to GROW UP, to know the whole truth and tell it in love—like Christ in everything. We take our lead from Christ, who is the source of everything we do. He keeps us in step with each other. His very breath and blood flow through us, nourishing us so that we will grow up healthy in God, robust in love. (Emphasis added)

Our (Erin, Greg, and Gary's) prayer is that through this book you were strengthened and encouraged to be responsible for your own thoughts, actions, feelings, and behaviors regardless of what your husband is or is not doing. That way you can have the greatest impact on your marriage. Your marriage may or may not be what you expected—and yet you can continue to stand true to your marriage commitment. Sometimes we end up in unexpected and even difficult places. In the poem "Welcome to Holland," Emily Perl Kingsley uses an extended metaphor to describe life's unpredictability. The poem compares expecting a baby to planning a trip to Italy. Kingsley notes that sometimes parenthood takes a turn and you wind up in Holland instead. Kingsley wrote, "If you spend your life mourning the fact that you didn't get to Italy, you may never be free to enjoy the very special, the very lovely things . . . about Holland."

Marriage may be different than what you thought you were signing up for. There may have been disappointments, unmet expectations, or even deep hurts that have left you broken-hearted. However, amid all of this you may have also been deeply blessed with times of laughter, intimacy, deep connection, and personal growth beyond what you ever imagined. Your marriage may not look like your parents', your best friend's, your neighbor's, or even your daughter's. But it is "your marriage."

You might currently be in a season of your marriage that feels joyful and connected. Enjoy and foster that gift! But when you pass through a season of challenge it may be easy to look around and say, "I wish that my husband was like hers" or "I wish that my marriage was like theirs." That's when it becomes easy to miss out on the beautiful thing that is happening right before your eyes. It's easy to get your eyes off of what God is doing, what He's teaching you and how He's growing you in your own situation. But don't miss out on the gift God has for you. If you find yourself in a hard place in your marriage, I encourage you to follow the advice of Emily Perl Kingsley and allow yourself to grieve whatever it was that you had expected and begin the process of embracing what God is doing right before you. What kind of wife is He growing you into right here and now—as a result of your situation? Are you being stretched because of personality differences? Are you learning how to honor your husband regardless of how you feel? Are you learning how to embrace the gift of sexual intimacy in your marriage? Is the Lord teaching you to trust Him more deeply through a season of waiting for a prayer to be answered?

◇◇◇◇◇◇◇◇◇◇◇◇◇◇◇◇◇◇◇◇◇◇◇ ♥ ♥ ♥ ◇◇◇◇◇◇◇◇◇◇◇◇◇◇◇◇◇◇◇◇◇◇◇

As long as you look to God as the source of all you want to see happen in your husband and your marriage, you don't have to be concerned about how it will happen. It's your job to pray. It's God's job to answer. Leave it in His hands.

—Stormie Omartian, *The Power of a Praying Wife*

◇◇◇◇◇◇◇◇◇◇◇◇◇◇◇◇◇◇◇◇◇◇◇ ♥ ♥ ♥ ◇◇◇◇◇◇◇◇◇◇◇◇◇◇◇◇◇◇◇◇◇◇◇

It's important to surround ourselves with a community of women who will support us through the difficult times and celebrate with us during the seasons of joy—we will experience both in marriage. Maybe you will find these other women by starting or joining a Wholehearted Wife group or maybe in a best friend, a sister, or even your mother. That's where I found encouragement and inspiration—my mother, whom I loved dearly. She was a role model for the type of wife I want to be. No, her marriage wasn't perfect; yet when all was said and done, she was remembered for loving her family wholeheartedly. What is it that you desire to be remembered for? When you stand before the throne of God, what it is you want to leave behind as your legacy?

At my mother's funeral several years ago my brother read an amazing tribute. He recalled her quirks and her legacy of loving, serving, and being faithful. That's what I want to be remembered for, even if things are challenging—that I stayed true to my word and stayed true to those I promised to be with for a lifetime—my husband and my family.

Here is what my brother shared about Mom:

I just wanted to take a few moments to tell you a few things about my mom. First of all, you're all probably aware that she was a very private, unassuming person who never wanted to draw any attention to herself. I can only imagine that if she knew that we were making such a fuss about her today (and take this with the spirit intended) she would just die.

My mom believed that everything is better with butter. From a bologna sandwich to broccoli, it just wasn't ready to eat until it was slathered in butter.

Mom believed in pretty much every old wives' tale that ever was. She would never let my sister and [me] near water until exactly one hour after eating, so fearful that we would get cramps.

She was incredibly superstitious . . . and a *huge* Phoenix Suns fan. When we were all watching a basketball game, I wasn't allowed to say anything bad about the team because I might jinx them . . . And I wasn't allowed to say anything too good about the team, because I might jinx them . . . Even though I thought she was crazy, the Suns have yet to win a championship; maybe she was right.

Mom believed that life is better with animals. She loved every dog, cat, rabbit, fish, and bird that [came] into the yard *dearly*.

She was the queen of coupons and rebates. She would drive all over town to hit every sale just to avoid paying retail prices on anything.

After working as a 9-1-1 operator for twenty years, Mom had come to love and respect officers of the law. Any time there was a report of an officer hurt or killed, Mom took it personally . . . someone that she cared about had been harmed.

Mom was a pretty cool mom, but I think that she was an even better grandma.

Larissa, Hannah, Taylor, Murphy, Garrison and Annie . . . your grandma loved you all so much. I hope that you cherish every moment you were able to spend with her.

The gospel of Matthew tells us that Jesus did not come to this earth to be served, but to serve others. My mother modeled Christ with an amazing servant's heart. At even the simplest of family gatherings, she was always the last one to eat because she was always making sure that everyone else had what they needed.

Philippians 2:3 says to think of others as better than yourselves . . . my mother lived by that.

Mom had rules. I know because I broke all of them before I left home. The one rule that she never wavered on was that you have to go to church. It didn't matter if it was a freezing North Dakota winter or a sweltering Arizona August . . . you go to church. In the last several weeks, the cancer started to deteriorate her mind, and even though she wasn't tracking everything in her head, I know she was in her heart. On Easter Sunday she seemed a little agitated. It occurred to me later that day that it might have been the first Easter that she had ever missed church.

Lastly, mom was an amazing fighter. She chose to fight cancer very privately, but she fought and fought and fought. Even in her greatest moments of fear she stayed so courageous.

So, what did I learn from my mom?

- Don't swim until one hour after you eat.
- Don't bad-mouth your team.
- Don't ever pay retail.
- Love and serve your family
- Fight for your life until the bitter end.
- And when all else fails, go to church . . . and cover everything with lots of butter.

What is it you want to leave with your husband and children—if today was the end? What have you gained through *The Wholehearted Wife* that could help you get there? Is there anything that has equipped you to love better, to show up differently, to communicate more effectively? Whatever it is, embrace it and utilize it.

*Let us not lose heart in doing good, for in due
time we will reap if we do not grow weary.*

—Galatians 6:9, NASB

This morning I (Erin) sat down with my cup of coffee and picked up a couples' devotional sitting next to my chair by the fireplace. As I began to read, I was reminded again that we as wives have so much influence over the temperature in our marriages. Stormie Omartian mirrors this truth in the following prayer:

Lord, I confess the times I've been unloving, critical, angry, resentful, disrespectful, or unforgiving toward my husband. Help me to put aside any hurt, anger, or disappointment I feel and forgive him the way You do—totally and completely, no looking back. Make me a tool of reconciliation, peace, and healing in this marriage. Make me my husband's helpmate, companion, champion, friend, and support. Help me to create a peaceful, restful, safe place for him to come to. Teach me how to take care of myself and stay attractive to him. Grow me into a creative and confident woman who is rich in mind, soul, and spirit. Make me the kind of woman he can be proud to say is his wife.[2]

I've prayed this prayer several times today. What a reminder of the rich privilege and important role we have as wives to love, honor, and encourage our husbands!

As you seek to fulfill this role in your marriage, remember to use the keys we've explored in this book. Each key can open the door to a more intimate, loving relationship with your husband and empower you to become the wholehearted wife described so well in Proverbs 31:11–12 (NLT):

> *Her husband can trust her*
> *and she will greatly enrich his life.*
> *She brings him good, not harm,*
> *all the days of her life.*

As we say our good-byes, we pray blessings on your husband and on your marriage and on you as you continue to journey toward becoming a wholehearted wife.

Acknowledgments

♥ ♥ ♥

This book could not have been completed without the help of my family, friends, and colleagues.

Thank you to my husband, Greg, for being a constant source of encouragement. You have been such an amazing gift from God. You constantly surprise me with the generosity, compassion, and love that you offer to me and our family.

Thank you to my children—Taylor, Murphy, Garrison, and Annie—who have been enormously patient with me during the long process of writing and rewriting this book. It is such an honor to be your mother. You have brought more meaning, excitement, and joy to my life than I ever knew was possible.

Thank you to my fabulous editors at Focus on the Family, Marianne Hering and Jennifer Lonas. You have helped bring this project to a whole new level. You both are amazing editors and have such wisdom to offer. It has been a joy to work with you.

Thank you to my friend and collaborator, Lisa Frieden. Truly, God allowed our paths to cross for "such a time as this." I know that you saved many of my brain cells throughout this process as you handled so many of the details. Thank you for doing this not just as another job, but as a ministry that you engaged with wholeheartedly.

Thank you to many at Focus on the Family, especially within the Marriage and Family Formation Division. Thank you for speaking into this project.

Thank you, Focus, for sharing my passion to help strengthen marriages and for continuing to fight for healthy families.

And, finally, thank you to the teams at Focus on the Family and Tyndale Publishing who have assisted with copyediting, internal design and layout, cover design, marketing, and the numerous details that are required to bring this book to press.

Notes

Introduction

1. Finding from a 2011 study by the Families and Work Institute, cited in Kenneth Matos and Ellen Galinsky, *Workplace Flexibility in the United States: A Status Report* (New York: Families and Work Institute, 2011), 12; http://familiesandwork.org/downloads/WorkplaceFlexibilityinUS.pdf.
2. Harris poll conducted October 16–19, 2008, cited in Harris Interactive, "Leisure Time Plummets 20 Percent in 2008—Hits New Low," December 4, 2008, http://www.harrisinteractive.com/vault/Harris-Interactive-Poll-Research-Time-and-Leisure-2008-12.pdf.
3. Statistics from the 2012 Stress in America survey, cited in "Stress by Gender," American Psychological Association, accessed December 14, 2013, http://www.apa.org/news/press/releases/stress/2012/gender-report.pdf.
4. Dictionary.com, s.v. "influence," accessed April 4, 2014, http://dictionary.reference.com/browse/influence.
5. Linda Dillow, *What's It Like to Be Married to Me?* (Colorado Springs: David C Cook, 2011), 32.

Key One

1. John Gottman and Nan Silver, *The Seven Principles for Making Marriage Work* (New York: Three Rivers Press, 1999), 63.

2. *Honor* as defined by Gary Smalley, Smalley Relationship Center, cited in Gary Smalley, "The Incredible Worth of a Wife," July 23, 2011, Crosswalk.com, http://www.crosswalk.com /family/marriage/the-incredible-worth-of-a-wife-11559591.html.

3. Greg Smalley and Gary Smalley, *Winning Your Husband Back Before It's Too Late* (Nashville: Thomas Nelson, 1999), 86.

4. Ibid., 87.

5. Robert S. McGee, *The Search for Significance* (Nashville: Thomas Nelson, 1998, 2003), 304.

6. Smalley, *Winning Your Husband Back Before It's Too Late*, 39–41.

7. BeNeca Ward, *Third Generation Country: A Practical Guide to Raising Children with Great Values* (USA: Xlibris, 2009), 119.

8. "Stradivarius Violin Price," Stradivarius.org, http://www .stradivarius.org/price; "Price of Stradivarius Violins," Stradivarius Violins, http://www.stradivariusviolins.org/pricesof stradivariusviolins.html.

9. Smalley, *Winning Your Husband Back Before It's Too Late*, 89.

10. Adapted from Gary Smalley, *Making Love Last Forever* (Nashville: Thomas Nelson, 1996), 185-196.

11. Allan V. Horwitz, Helene R. White, and Sandra Howell-White, "Becoming Married and Mental Health: A Longitudinal Study of a Cohort of Young Adults," *Journal of Marriage and Family* 58, no. 4 (November 1996): 895–907.

12. Scott J. South and Kyle D. Crowder, "Escaping Distressed Neighborhoods: Individual, Community, and Metropolitan Influences," *American Journal of Sociology* 102, no. 4 (January 1997): 1040–84.

13. Kate Antonovics and Robert Town, "Are All the Good Men Married? Uncovering the Sources of the Marital Wage Premium," *American Economic Review* 94, no. 2 (May 2004):

317–21; Daniel T. Lichter, Deborah Roempke, and Brian J. Brown, "Is Marriage a Panacea? Union Formation Among Economically Disadvantaged Unwed Mothers," *Social Problems* 50, no. 1 (February 2003): 60–86.

14. Corey L. M. Keyes, "Social Civility in the United States," *Sociological Inquiry* 72, no. 3 (Summer 2002): 393–408.

15. Stephanie A. Bond Huie, Robert A. Hummer, and Richard G. Rogers, "Individual and Contextual Risks of Death Among Race and Ethnic Groups in the United States," *Journal of Health and Social Behavior* 43, no. 3 (September 2002): 359–81.

16. Christopher F. Scott and Susan Sprecher, "Sexuality in Marriage, Dating, and Other Relationships: A Decade Review," *Journal of Marriage and Family* 62, no. 4 (November 2000): 999–1017.

Key Two

1. Adapted from Gary Smalley, *The DNA of Relationships: Discover How You Are Designed for Satisfying Relationships* (Carol Stream, IL: Tyndale, 2004), 114.

Key Three

1. Personality profile developed in cooperation with John Trent. Adapted from Gary Smalley and John Trent, *The Two Sides of Love* (Carol Stream, IL: Tyndale, 2006).

2. Barna Group, "Three Trends on Faith, Work and Calling," February 11, 2014, accessed March 15, 2014, https://www.barna .org/barna-update/culture/649-three-major-faith-and-culture -trends-for-2014#.UyYOtChQY5Q. Used with permission.

3. If accepting yourself is an area of struggle, read Psalm 139 and thank God aloud every day for the way He designed you.

4. Charles R. Swindoll, *Standing Out* (Portland: Multnomah, 1983), 51–53.

5. Shelley E. Taylor, Laura C. Klein, Brian P. Lewis, Tara L. Gruenewald, Regan A. R. Gurung, and John. A. Updegraff, "Biobehavioral Responses to Stress in Females: Tend-and-Befriend, Not Fight-or-Flight," *Psychological Review* 107, no. 3 (July 2000): 411–29.

Key Four

1. *Strong's Concordance*, s.v. Greek 4125 *pneumatikos*, accessed March 17, 2014, http://www.blueletterbible.org/lang/Lexicon /Lexicon.cfm?strongs=G4152&t=NASB.

2. *Blue Letter Bible* website defines *spiritual* as "relating to the human spirit, or rational soul, as part of the man which is akin to God and serves as his instrument or organ." Accessed March 17, 2014, http://www.blueletterbible.org/lang/Lexicon/Lexicon .cfm?strongs=G4152&t=NASB.

3. Judy Bodmer, "Reluctant Leader: Help Your Husband Become the Spiritual Leader of Your Home," JudyBodmer.com, accessed December 29, 2013, http://judybodmer.com/?page_id=46.

4. On an average Sunday, 17.8 percent of US men and 25.3 percent of US women attend church. Data found in The Association of Religion Data Archives survey "American Time Use Survey, 2010," http://thearda.com/Archive/Files/Descriptions/ ATUS2010.asp. Interpretation of the data found in Stanley Presser and Mark Chaves, "Is Religious Service Attendance Declining?" *Journal for the Scientific Study of Religion*, 46(3):417-423 and Mark Chaves, *American Religion: Contemporary Trends* (Princeton, NJ: Princeton University Press, 2011), 44. Census information by Lindsay M. Howden and Julie A. Meyer, "Age

and Sex Composition: 2010," May 2011, http://www.census.gov/prod/cen2010/briefs/c2010br-03.pdf. The 2010 US census data reports there are roughly 109 million men and 116 million women, which yields a difference in weekly church attendance between US men and women of about 10 million.

5. Cynthia Woolever and Deborah Bruce, *A Field Guide to U.S. Congregations: Who's Going Where and Why*, 2nd ed., (Westminster: John Knox Press, 2010) 15.

6. From "The American Time Use Survey, 2010." See note 4.

7. Barna Research Online, "Women Are the Backbone of Christian Congregations in America," March 6, 2000, www.barna.org, cited in David Murrow, *Why Men Hate Going to Church* (Nashville: Thomas Nelson, 2005), 8.

8. Based on a show of hands at the National Coalition of Men's Ministries meeting in 2005. Adapted from Murrow, "Quick Facts," http://churchformen.com/men-and-church/where-are-the-men/.

9. Chris Sprad, "What to Do When Your Spouse Doesn't Spiritually Lead the Family," EpicParent.TV, September 28, 2011, http://www.epicparent.tv/what-to-do-when-your-spouse-doesnt-spiritually-lead-the-family/.

10. John Piper, "What Should a Wife Do When Her Husband Doesn't Lead Spiritually?" DesiringGod.org, June 20, 2008, http://www.desiringgod.org/resource-library/ask-pastor-john/what-should-a-wife-do-when-her-husband-doesnt-lead-spiritually.

11. Thirty-Day Husband Encouragement Challenge, May 4, 2011, Revive Our Hearts, accessed December 29, 2013, http://www.reviveourhearts.com/articles/30-day-husband-encouragement-challenge/.

12. Allison Stevens, "What Does It Mean for a Wife to Submit to Her Husband?" Questions.org, RBC Ministries, accessed December 29, 2013, http://questions.org/attq/what-does -it-mean-for-a-wife-to-submit-to-her-husband/.

13. Adapted from Dan Lacich, "Provocative Bible Verses: Wives Submit to Your Husbands," October 12, 2009, http://provoca- tivechristian.wordpress.com/2009/10/12/provocative-bible -verses-wives-submit-to-your-husbands/.

14. *Strong's Concordance*, s.v. Greek 5293, *hupotasso*, accessed March 18, 2014, http://www.studylight.org/lex/grk/gwview .cgi?n=5293.

15. Adapted from Mary Kassian, "Seven Misconceptions About Submission," Girls Gone Wise, November 15, 2011, http:// www.girlsgonewise.com/7-misconceptions-about-submission/.

16. Ibid.

17. For more encouragement, check out Lynn and Dineen's blog at http://www.spirituallyunequalmarriage.com/. Quote from Lynn Donovan, Dineen Miller, and Darla Stone, interview by Dennis Rainey and Bob Lepine, *Family Life Today*, radio broad- cast, December 4, 2012, http://www.familylife.com/audio /topics/marriage/challenges/spiritually-mismatched/married-to -an-unbeliever/20121204-when-differing-values-collide.

18. Adapted from "How Do You Encourage Your Husband to Lead, Spiritually?" Circle of Moms discussion board, April 13, 2010, http://www.circleofmoms.com/christian-mommies/how -do-you-encourage-your-husband-to-lead-spiritually-520694.

19. Stormie Omartian, *The Power of a Praying Wife* (Eugene, OR: Harvest House, 1997), 29.

20. David M. Schnarch, *Constructing the Sexual Crucible: An Integration of Sexual and Marital Therapy* (New York: W. W. Norton, 1991), 121.

21. Gary J. Oliver, Ph.D., Executive Director of The Center for Relationship Enrichment at John Brown University, first developed the chart in the late 1990s for use in graduate theological studies, seminars, and workshops; Dr. Oliver continues to update the concept and the categories.

22. Mark Batterson, *Wild Goose Chase* (Colorado Springs: Multnomah, 2008), 50.

23. Survey published in Christopher G. Ellison, Amy M. Burdette, and W. Bradford Wilcox, "The Couple That Prays Together: Race and Ethnicity, Religion, and Relationship Quality Among Working-Age Adults," *Journal of Marriage and Family* 72, no. 4 (August 2010): 963–75.

Key Five

1. Survey results published in Gary Smalley, *Making Love Last Forever* (Nashville: Thomas Nelson, 1996), 141.

2. John Powell, *Why Am I Afraid to Tell You Who I Am?* (Great Britain: Fount Paperbacks, 1999), 2.

3. Ibid., 2–3.

4. *Connie Grigsby,* quoted in Belinda Elliot, "Get Your Husband to Listen to You," CBN.com, accessed March 18, 2014, http://www.cbn.com/family/marriage/elliott_husbandslisten.aspx.

5. Your Tango Experts/Richard Drobnick, "Six Ways Men and Women Communicate Differently," PsychCentral.com, 2012, accessed December 31, 2013, http://psychcentral.com/blog/archives/2012/04/01/6-ways-men-and-women-communicate-differently/.

6. Marianne J. Legato, "How to Talk to a Man," Prevention.com, December 2011, accessed December 31, 2013, http://www.prevention.com/health/sex-relationships/how-talk-man.

7. Cited in John Gottman, *The Seven Principles for Making Marriage Work* (New York: Three Rivers Press, 1999), 27.

8. Connie Grigsby, quoted in Belinda Elliott, "Get Your Husband to Listen to You," CBN.com, accessed March 18, 2013, http://www.cbn.com/family/marriage/elliott_husbandslisten.aspx.

9. Material adapted from Gary Smalley, *Hidden Keys to Loving Relationships*, (Branson, MO: American Telecast and Smalley Relationship Center, 2003); Gary Smalley, *Secrets to Lasting Love*, (New York: Fireside, 2000), chapter 1; Gary Smalley, *Making Love Last Forever*, (Thomas Nelson, 1996), chapter 9. Gary Smalley based the material in these books on John Powell, *Why Am I Afraid to Tell You Who I Am?* (Fount, 1999), chapter 9; interviews in 1982 with Dr. Gary J. Oliver; and David Mace, *Love and Anger in Marriage* (Zondervan, 1984), chapter 8.

10. Sari Harrar and Rita DeMaria, *The 7 Stages of Marriage* (Pleasantville, NY: Reader's Digest Books, 2007)

Key Six

1. Gary Smalley explained this term in (Nashville: Thomas Nelson, 1996), ch

2. Ibid.

3. See Nick Stinnett and John DeFrain, *Se ... amilies* (New York: Little, Brown and Company, 1986), 101–102.

4. Ed Wheat and Gaye Wheat, *Intended for Pleasure*, 4th ed. (Grand Rapids: Revell, 2010), 14.

5. Linda Dillow and Lorraine Pintus, *Intimate Issues: Twenty-One Questions Christian Women Ask About Sex* (Colorado Springs: WaterBrook, 1999), 68–69.

6. Sheila Wray Gregoire, *The Good Girl's Guide to Great Sex* (Grand Rapids: Zondervan, 2012), 194–195.

7. Sheila Wray Gregoire, "Twenty-Nine Days to Great Sex: Day 9: Preparing for Sex Throughout the Day," *To Love, Honor, and Vacuum* (blog), February 9, 2012, http://tolovehonor andvacuum.com/2012/02/29-days-to-great-sex-day-9-preparing -for-sex-throughout-the-day/.

8. Juli Slattery, *No More Headaches: Enjoying Sex and Intimacy in Marriage* (Carol Stream, IL: Tyndale, 2009), 100–101.

9. David Bentley, "Everything You Always Wanted to Know About Men," Bentley Marriage and Family Counseling, 2011, accessed January 1, 2014, http://denver-marriage-counseling .com/2011/03/understanding-men/.

10. Slattery, *No More Headaches*, 112.

11. Sharon Cohen, "Appreciate Your Husband's Sex Drive," *Your Husband's Deepest Desire* (blog), July 28, 2010, accessed January 1, 2014, http://husbandsdeepestdesire .blogspot.com/2010/07/appreciate-your-husbands-sex-drive .html.

12. Shaunti Feldhahn, *For Women Only: What You Need to Know About the Inner Lives of Men* (Colorado Springs: Multnomah, 2013), 117.

13. Paul Byerley, quoted in Sheila Wray Gregoire, "Twenty-Nine Days to Great Sex: Day 6: Why Your Hubby Wants Your Body," *To Love, Honor, and Vacuum* (blog), February 6, 2012, accessed January 2, 2014, http://tolovehonorandvacuum.com /2012/02/29-days-to-great-sex-day-6-why-your-hubby-wants -your-body/.

14. Slattery, *No More Headaches*, 105.

15. Dillow and Pintus, *Intimate Issues*, 68–69.

16. Dave Currie, "Help! My Husband Doesn't Want Sex!," Sex and Love, PowertoChange.com, 2012, accessed January 2,

2014, http://powertochange.com/sex-love/nosex/comment
-page-25/.

17. John Eldredge, *Wild at Heart: Discovering the Secret of a Man's Soul* (Nashville: Thomas Nelson, 2010), 15–16.

18. Slattery, *No More Headaches*, 107.

19. Ibid., 114–5.

20. Interview with Juli Slattery, Colorado Springs, Colorado, December 2012.

21. The Focus on the Family counseling department recommends the information posted on their website, *Pureintimacy.org*. Other helpful books are listed at the following site: http://media.focusonthefamily.com/topicinfo/overcoming_sexual _brokenness.pdf.

22. Mark Schoen, quoted in "Marriage and Sex," Love and Relationships, DiscoveryHealth.com, accessed January 2, 2014, http://health.howstuffworks.com/relationships/marriage /marriage-and-sex-dictionary.htm.

23. Ibid.

24. Review of studies on sex, cited in "Is Love Better for Men's or Women's Health?," Health.com, June 3, 2012, http://magazine .foxnews.com/food-wellness/love-better-mens-or-womens -health.

25. Denise A. Donnelly, "Sexually Inactive Marriages," *Journal of Sex Research* 30, no. 2 (1993): 171.

26. David G. Blanchflower and Andrew J. Oswald, "Money, Sex, and Happiness: An Empirical Study," *Scandinavian Journal of Economics* 106, no. 3 (September 2004): 393–415.

27. *Strong's Concordance*, s.v. Hebrew 3045, *yada*, accessed March 18, 2014, http://www.studylight.org/lex/heb/hwview .cgi?n=03045.

28. Paraphrased from Slattery, *No More Headaches*, 44–49.

Key Seven

1. Concepts discussed in Gary Smalley, *Hidden Keys to Loving Relationships Study Guide* (Siloam Springs, AR: Northwest Arkansas Healthy Marriages, 1993), 52.

2. Some of the discussion on buttons appears in Greg Smalley, *Fight Your Way to a Better Marriage* (New York: Howard, 2012), 24–33.

3. Ibid., 28.

4. Ibid., 28–29.

5. Adapted from Greg Smalley, *Fight Your Way to a Better Marriage*, 30.

6. Adapted from Greg Smalley, Erin Smalley, and John Michael, *Hearts Restored: A Transformational 3-day Marriage Experience* (Colorado Springs: Focus on the Family, 2012), 11–13.

7. Adapted from Greg Smalley, *Fight Your Way to a Better Marriage*, 172.

8. John Gottman, *Why Marriages Succeed or Fail and How You Can Make Yours Last* (New York: Simon and Schuster, 1994), 179.

9. Matthew D. Lieberman et al., "Putting Feelings into Words: Affect Labeling Disrupts Amygdala Activity in Response to Affective Stimuli," *Psychological Science* 18, no. 5 (May 2007): 421–28.

10. Henry Cloud and John Townsend, *Boundaries in Marriage* (Grand Rapids: Zondervan, 1999), 170-75.

11. Adapted from Greg Smalley, *Fight Your Way to a Better Marriage*, 29. Original study is Lauren M. Papp, E. Mark Cummings, and Marcie C. Goeke-Morey, "For Richer, for Poorer: Money as a Topic of Marital Conflict in the Home," *Family Relations: Interdisciplinary Journal of Applied Family Studies,* 58, no. 1 (February 2009): 58, 100.

12. Adapted from Gary Smalley, *Making Love Last Forever* (Nashville: Thomas Nelson, 1996), 215–17.

13. Adapted from Smalley, *Fight Your Way to a Better Marriage*, 212–221.

Key Eight

1. Sandra Thomas, quoted in Melissa Dittmann, "Anger Across the Gender Divide," *Monitor on Psychology* 34, no. 3 (March 2003): 52, http://www.apa.org/monitor/mar03/angeracross.aspx.

2. Adapted from Drs. H. Norman Wright and Gary J. Oliver, *A Woman's Forbidden Emotion* (Ventura, CA: Regal, 2005), 90.

3. Gary Smalley, *Making Love Last Forever* (Nashville: Thomas Nelson, 1996), 19.

4. Ross Campbell, *How to Really Love Your Child* (Colorado Springs: Chariot Victor, 1992), 84.

5. Gary Smalley, *Keys to Loving Relationships Study Guide* (Siloam Springs, AR: Northwest Arkansas Healthy Marriages, 1993), 60.

6. "Mental Health and Anger Management," Mental Health Center, WebMD.com, February 18, 2012, accessed January 5, 2014, http://www.webmd.com/mental-health/anger-management.

7. Smalley, *Keys to Loving Relationships Study Guide*, 60.

8. Wright and Oliver, *A Woman's Forbidden Emotion*, 161.

9. Based on concepts presented in Georgia Shaffer, *Taking Out Your Emotional Trash* (Eugene, OR: Harvest House, 2010), 82-85.

10. Post from a discussion board on TalkAboutMarriage.com, August 2010, accessed January 8, 2014, http://talkaboutmarriage.com/general-relationship-discussion/16185-please-help-how-deal-my-husbands-temper.html.

11. Quoted and paraphrased from Greg and Erin Smalley, Q&A response, "Enriching Relationships for a Lifetime," Center for Relationship Enrichment, January 8, 2014, http://life relationships.com/resources/qa/viewAnswer.asp?articleid=140 &categoryid=22.

12. Wright and Oliver, *A Woman's Forbidden Emotion*, 171.

13. Quoted in Carol Tavris, *Anger: The Misunderstood Emotion* (New York: Touchstone, 1989), 221.

14. Gary Smalley, *Keys to Loving Relationships Study Guide* (Branson, MO: Smalley Relationship Center, 2005), 10.

Key Nine

1. "Can You Forgive Lance Armstrong? *USA Today*, January 18, 2013, http://www.usatoday.com/story/news/nation/2013 /01/17/forgive-lance-armstrong-redemption/1843073/.

2. Ibid.

3. Ibid.

4. Erin Smalley and Carrie Oliver, *Grown-Up Girlfriends* (Carol Stream, IL: Tyndale, 2007), 133.

5. See Gary Smalley, *Keys to Loving Relationships Study Guide* (Branson, MO: Smalley Relationship Center, 2005), 62.

6. An excellent book that addresses this topic is *Lies Women Believe and the Truth That Sets Them Free* by Nancy Leigh DeMoss (Chicago: Moody, 2001).

7. Lewis B. Smedes, *Shame and Grace* (New York: HarperCollins, 1993), 136, 141.

8. Based on list in *Keys to Loving Relationships Study Guide*, 64–68.

9. Henry Cloud and John Townsend, *Boundaries in Marriage* (Grand Rapids: Zondervan, 1999), 137.

10. Adapted from *The Marriage Course Manual* (New York: AAP Publishing, 2008), 48–55.

Key Ten

1. C. S. Lewis, *The Problem of Pain* (New York: Macmillan, 1962), 93.
2. Gary Smalley, *Your Relationship with God: Drawing Closer to God Every Day* (Carol Stream, IL: Tyndale, 2006), 88.
3. Treasure-hunting steps and discussion are based on Gary Smalley's book *Your Relationship with God* (pages 90–92) and the DVD series *Hidden Keys to Loving Relationships* (DVD 3, session 10; Gary Smalley Seminars, 1993).
4. Paraphrased and adapted from Gary Smalley, *Making Love Last Forever* (Nashville: Thomas Nelson, 1996), 35–38.
5. Ibid., 38.
6. *It's a Wonderful Life*, directed by Frank Capra, Liberty Films/RKO Radio Pictures, 1946.
7. John Piper, *Desiring God*, rev. ed. (Colorado Springs: Multnomah, 2011), 265.
8. Dennis Rainey, "How Can I Keep My Family Strong in the Midst of Tragedy and Suffering," FamilyLife.com, accessed January 11, 2014, http://www.familylife.com/articles/topics/marriage/challenges/hardship-and-suffering/how-can-i-keep-my-family-strong-in-the-midst-of-tragedy-and-suffering.
9. Ibid.
10. Mary Beth Chapman, *Choosing to See: A Journey of Struggle and Hope* (Grand Rapids: Revell, 2010).
11. To learn more of Corrie's story, read *The Hiding Place* (Grand Rapids: Chosen Books, 2006) and *Tramp for the Lord* (Fort Washington, PA: Christian Literature Crusade, 2008).

Conclusion

1. Emily Perl Kingsley, "Welcome to Holland," © 1987. See National Congress for Down Syndrome, http://www.ndsc

center.org/resources/new-and-expectant-parents/welcome-to
-holland/.

2. Stormie Omartian, *A Book of Prayers for Couples* (Eugene, OR: Harvest House, 2011), 10.

Meet the rest of the family

Expert advice on parenting and marriage . . .
spiritual growth . . . powerful personal stories . . .

Focus on the Family's collection of inspiring, practical resources can help your family grow closer to God—and each other—than ever before. Whichever format you need—video, audio, book or eBook—we have something for you. Visit our online Family Store and discover how we can help your family thrive at **FocusOnTheFamily.com/resources.**